The Goddess' Guide to Love

TIMELESS SECRETS TO DIVINE ROMANCE

Margie Lapanja

Margie Lapanja

CONARI PRESS
Berkeley, California

The author gratefully acknowledges permission to excerpt from the following works:
"Cassidy" by The Grateful Dead, words by John Barlow. Copyright 1972, Ice Nine
Publishing Company, Inc. All Rights Reserved. Used by permission of Ice Nine
Publishing Company, Inc. "Sugar Magnolia" by The Grateful Dead, words by Robert
Hunter. Copyright 1970, Ice Nine Publishing Company, Inc. All Rights Reserved. Used
by permission of Ice Nine Publishing Company, Inc. "Sunrise" by The Grateful Dead,
words by Donna Godchaux. Copyright 1977, Ice Nine Publishing Company, Inc. All
Rights Reserved. Used by permission of Ice Nine Publishing Company, Inc. *Goddess in
the Kitchen* by Margie Lapanja. Copyright 1998 by Margie Beiser Lapanja.
Reprinted with permission of Conari Press.

Conari Press books are distributed by Publishers Group West.

Cover design: *Martha Newton Furman Design & Illustration*
Cover illustration: *Return of Spring* by William Adolphe Bouguereau.
Reprinted by permission of Joslyn Art Museum, Omaha, Nebraska
Cover art direction: *Ame Beanland*
Book design: *Suzanne Albertson*

ISBN: 1-57324-143-1

Library of Congress Cataloging-in-Publication Data
Lapanja, Margie, 1959–
The goddess' guide to love : timeless secrets to divine romance / Margie Lapanja.
p.   cm.
Includes bibliographical references and index.
ISBN 1-57324-143-1 (trade paper)
1. Man-woman relationships. 2. Love. 3. Sex. 4. Cookery for two. I. Title.
HQ801.L298 1999   98–45503
306.7—dc21   CIP

Printed in the United States of America on recycled paper.

98 99 00 01   DATA REPRO   10 9 8 7 6 5 4 3 2 1

She's a summer love
in the spring, fall, and winter
She can make happy any man alive

—"Sugar Magnolia"
The Grateful Dead, words by Robert Hunter

Goddess' Guide to Love

FOREWORD

My copy of The Goddess' Guide to Love is so marked up with my highlighting the sections I love that the book nearly glows yellow like the sun. How appropriate for a book that sheds light and delight on the topic of love. You're not going to like this book—you're going to *cherish* this book.

Margie Lapanja presents deep Truths ("It is our spiritual responsibility…to live in love"). She also writes in a sweeping, romantic manner ("To feel love, we must first feel the wind in our souls, the waterfall of our emotions, the fire in our bodies, and the earth under us as we sleep, dream, and dance"). As I first read this book I found myself exclaiming aloud numerous times ("Wow!" "What a great concept," "Tracey [my bride] will love this"). If you find yourself doing this too, go with it. Books can be a form of two-way communication. You'll get far more out of a book if you interact with it instead of simply reading it. In *The Goddess' Guide to Love*, there is ample opportunity to do just that.

I've always been entranced by "poetic prose"—the masterful tales of Ray Bradbury, the spiritual parables of Kahlil Gibran. I now add Margie Lapanja to this exclusive list. She has that rare knack of writing in an extravagant but not exaggerated manner. Her style is lush but not loud. My experience of reading *The Goddess' Guide to Love* was a curious combination of comfort and excitement. Perhaps this is what "magic" is. I think it's interesting that a man was asked to write the Foreword to this, a most feminine book. I look upon it as an honor. Since the focus of my work is the romantic aspect of love, my affinity and appreciation for Margie Lapanja's work is natural and expected. What I didn't expect was the number of wonderful "Ah-ha!" experiences this book gave me. For instance, I learned that I am a "Goddess-kissed" man (as opposed to a "Goddess-dissed" man). Margie says, "A goddess-kissed man has felt the embrace of the divine feminine at some point in his life." She's explained insightfully the creative and lasting influence my mother had on me. Margie describes mothers as "the first goddess" in our lives. Isn't that marvelous?

In addition to the many "Ah-ha's" this book has bestowed on me, it has also given me many "Uh-huh" exclamations of recognition, as I read Margie's magical explanations of concepts that I believe in deeply, have taught frequently, and have written about ("The secret to loving is loving"). Her unique viewpoint and wonderful way with words impresses me on every single page. Whether you have been with someone for six weeks or sixty years, you always hold the power to recreate the sensations and magic of any stage of love whenever you desire." Yes!) I confess that I often reacted by whispering wistfully, "I wish I'd written that." But I am truly glad that Margie has written it, and that you have picked up this book and are about to share in a glorious adventure.

This book is full of inspiration and encouragement. But it's not merely a "gee-whiz" kind of inspiration—it's something much deeper and more specific. There are many practical tips, things to do. This is terrific, because I believe that there is great power in taking action. There is also great power in concepts that help people to reconceive their lives and the world. *The Goddess' Guide to Love* is a wonderful collection of concepts that celebrate and explain love and the feminine experience and opportunities of love.

Margie has wrapped her book around the four seasons. My initial reaction was that it was a "great concept." But I came to appreciate that it is also integral, necessary, organic—feminine.

I admit to a little jealousy that some of the goddess' doors are closed to me. I can certainly appreciate all of the concepts herein—and I experience love, as love is a human emotion and not gender-based, as some would have you believe—but I cannot share the same experience as women. My body isn't tuned to the cycles of the moon, my creations are the product of my head and hands, and my emotions seem a little harder to access. (Ah, well, there are some masculine compensations!) But the feminine is wonderful, fascinating, and alluring. Revel in it. Celebrate it. Live it!

> Gregory J. P. Godek, husband, father,
> and author of *1001 Ways to Be Romantic*
> and *10,000 Ways to Say I Love You*

CHAPTER 1

The Call of the Goddess

If you want to be happy, be.

—LEO TOLSTOY

Answering Love's Call

Are you ready?

*A*t some moment during each human life, the heart and spirit are set aflame with an overwhelming, intoxicating desire to be free: surrender to the power of universal truth; return to the garden; drive down an open road with no map; backstroke down the river of life; relinquish all possessions, material and emotional; spring-clean the soul; release the past; embrace the present; create the future—to start anew and be free to love.

To ignite the divine fire within and let that love light shine, we must dare to lay down old defenses and explore our own beliefs and personal visions of love and freedom. If our hearts are open (and if we're receptive), we realize it is our spiritual responsibility to illuminate life with more playfulness, joy, wonder, and beauty, for it is our innate, natural, ancient birthright—as bright, wise, and wild children of the universe—to live in love. This epiphany shines through our souls, revealing a life of vibrancy and happiness.

And then we awaken from the dream. Oh, it felt so good, it sounded so beautiful, we were inspired and actually soaring with possibilities. But as we rub our eyes to clear our vision, our hearts are still hungry, our souls are still thirsty. How do we dance into this dream and free this love in our hearts? How do we create this inspiring, peaceful, and lasting love in our challenging, fast-forward lives?

The answer lies in putting on our rainbow-tinted goddess glasses and learning to see love in a fresh and redeemed light. We must dare to look up at the moon, nourish our psychic souls, and open our hearts to the divine power and mystery of the universal playground we call love. Then we can begin to transcend all the preconditioned definitions of love that have been poured into our minds over the years. By listening to the eternal heartbeat of the seasons—winter, spring, summer, and fall—and moving to the timeless tempo of natural law, we can discover the secrets of love's pulse and understand the answers to its riddles. For like the songs of the seasons, the phases of the moon, and the power of the elements that sustain life, love possesses its own rhythm, flawless and irresistible. To feel love, we must first feel the wind in our souls, the waterfall of our emotions, the fire in our bodies, and the earth under us as we sleep, dream, and dance.

The Seasons of Love
What is your favorite season?
Why is this season so special to you?

I have found that most people have a swift, enthusiastic answer to these two questions. Something in you seems to vibrate to a particular season, as if the essence of summer or spring or fall or winter is actually in your DNA. Maybe childhood memories have imprinted an everlasting sentiment of the love, laughter, and fun of a certain time of the year. Maybe you were born during that time; a summer baby who as an adult now enjoys basking in the long, languid days of August eating watermelon, or a child born in midwinter who now counts the days until the ski slopes open.

Perhaps you experienced your first breath of love in spring. If so, do you still relish the feeling of a playful April breeze, or does the sight of the runoff water from the melting snows make your heart quicken? Ask yourself again and really give the question focus:

What is your favorite season?
Why do you enjoy it so?

Now, shut your eyes and think about love. Love. *Love*. Consider love as it moves through stages or "seasons" of its own, complete with all the feelings, colors, wonders, and celebrations that make our earthly seasons unique. What season would you say your love is in now? Is it cool and quiet like winter? Steamy and passionate like summer? Enchanting and fresh like spring? Rich and colorful like autumn? Are you satisfied with the season of love you have created in your life at the moment? Or do you long for a different season of love?

Reflect for a moment on your present *love season*.
What are you learning in this season of love?

For a woman who honors the goddess-graced dance of life in its mystery and magnificence, love *does* have very tangible seasons of it own—love's Vision, Enchantment, Passion, and Celebration. A goddess allows love to flourish naturally—free of manipulation and constraint—where it is governed by the same universal and divine laws that make flowers bloom, rivers flow, and trees turn golden in fall's embrace. She knows to draw from the wisdom of Mother Nature's metaphors and uses this knowledge to enhance each stage of love as it occurs. You see, true love cannot be driven through a linear, start-to-finish course where two people meet, fall in love, marry, live together, and part at the end of their days. Rather, it must be free to flow and recede, flirt and retreat, and grow and rest in cycles as timeless and resplendent as the phases of the moon. In this state, love will endure in an unending circle of promise as a relationship evolves. This is the beauty and splendor of love.

In another light, whether you have been with someone for six weeks or sixty years, you always hold the power to recreate the sensations and magic of any stage of love whenever you desire. By invoking the secrets and gifts of each season, you can reignite the Passion of love, set the mood for lively Celebration, or restore the freshness and wonder of Enchantment at will.

To stir up Passion in my relationship, for example, I look to the full moon and perfume my body with summer scents like sandalwood, rose, and musk. I call on the lascivious spirit of the goddess Ishtar to guide me in her ancient wiles of pleasure. The colors, songs, and scents of spring can enliven the Enchantment in our lives. At other times, when I feel our marriage needs to be fortified with Vision and insight, I heed the wisdom of silence as reflected in the quiet of winter and turn inward with meditation and self-indulgent pampering. Our love thrives on the freshness of a new day, the energy and intensity of a spring thunderstorm, the charm of a quiet, moonlit night.

In the midst of winter I discovered within me an invincible summer.
—ALBERT CAMUS

The Goddess Rules

A goddess in love learns to transcend all worries of an outcome by drawing insight and confidence from the "precious present." Leave all of the marriage manipulation tactics to the "Rules Girls"; the goal for a Goddess Girl is not to coerce him into putting a wedding ring on your finger, but to inspire him to wrap an incandescent ring of love around *you*. A ring is a thoughtful and symbolic gift, certainly a charming accessory if you have beautiful hands, but a gift of someone's truest love is much more valuable.

However, I'm sure that many of you still have residual "rights and wrongs" floating about your psyches, leftovers from reading all those other books or listening to this or that friend as she expounds in ungoddess-like diatribes of what to do with this or that man. Society's—often your mother's, your father's, your therapist's, your priest's, even an old lover's—notion of what romantic love and the prospering relationship *should* be has left you feeling overwhelmed. You've been told what love is *supposed* to be, how it's *supposed* to feel, what you're *supposed* to do, and what rules *shouldn't* be broken.

Even the clichés used to describe the phases of love that are imbedded in our psyches lend skewed connotations. Are we destined to *look*—search, hunt—for love, or do we have the power to *attract* it? Do we really fall—descend, plummet, weaken—in love, or do we truly *ascend, float, soar?* Why do we strive to *stay*—halt! freeze!—in love when we should really *thrive* and *play* in love?

Via a simple semantic flight of fancy, clear your vision and look at love with a fresh and spirited perspective. For there are dynamics to happiness in love

that a wise goddess always keeps in focus and in motion. A goddess who is try-
ing to reconcile her heart's true desires amidst her body's hormonal demands
and her conditioned, whimsical notions of romance must always remember
and honor the *Goddess Rules of Love*.

The Goddess Rules of Love

1. Above all, a goddess does not *look* for love, she *attracts* love;
she does not *fall* in love, she *ascends* with love; and she feels
no pressure to *stay in love* when she knows she can forever
play in love! (And, since you are not inclined to *fall in* love, you
will never worry about *falling out* of love!)

2. Do what you love to do. "Follow your bliss," live your dreams,
listen to music that moves your soul, play with people you
like, aspire to do work you enjoy, and take excellent care of
yourself in the process.

3. Mortals' rules don't apply to goddesses. Strive to overcome the
nagging voice of the critic on your shoulder whispering all
the things that you are *supposed* to do. Define what is truly
best for you. "Take the best and leave the rest."

4. Learn to release gracefully and gratefully with divine timing. This
is what I call "giving (someone, a self-defeating habit, a dead-

end situation) back to the angels." There is always a defining moment—often in the midst of challenge—of insight and intuitive understanding when your situation is exposed in divine light. Take heed. As Winnie the Pooh said, "I've come to a very important decision—these are the wrong sorts of bee." Have faith. *Let go and let goddess*—allow nature to take her course. Something better awaits you.

> *Do what is nourishing to your spirit;*
> *do not do what is loathsome to your spirit.*
> —ALAN COHEN

At Play in the Fields of the Goddess

Just as every new dawn brings with it the promise of renewal and fulfillment, every encounter with that supreme and eternal force of life— *love*—holds another key to knowing it, feeling it, living it, being it. The secret to loving is loving. This is where the fun begins, for this is where the soulful, vibrant goddess-spirit within beckons: "Do you want to come out and play?"

This is the playground of the divine feminine, the cauldron of creation, a invitation to reclaim love in all of its mystery and magnificence. This is the circle of unending love, the untiring, blissful dance of grace and passion, born of infinite vitality where we reconnect to the rhythms and rhymes of life. By venerating these timeless secrets of the moon, nature, and the goddess within, we are assured divine romance.

It is here we reconnect with ourselves as women of sensual wisdom and intuitive vision, tempered with a tigress' dose of personal power. A goddess in love is a woman who accepts her gifts and lets her love shine. A goddess in love is a woman who, when confronted with troubling confines of values not her own, tosses her head back and fills hearts with her light and laughter. A goddess in love listens to the whisperings of her spirit, embraces life with an eagerness to explore and learn, and allows love in its many seasons to permeate her thoughts, actions, emotions, and choices. An artisan of the senses, she nourishes body and soul with her vibrance.

Choose Your Muse

Be your fantasy—the woman you admire
and revere—but stay true to yourself.
—BRENDA VENUS, *Secrets of Seduction for Women*

*A*s a very young goddess protégé, I recognized a model of mystical femininity in full regalia in Glinda, the Good Witch of the North, in *The Wizard of Oz*, when she waved her star-tipped wand over the Wicked Witch of the West and chuckled, "You have no power here. Be gone! . . ." And smiling with hers eyes, she hugged Dorothy and floated away in her glorious way. Glinda radiated serenity, security, and wisdom—to this day, one of my favorite visions of a woman at ease with herself and the magic she commands.

Who inspires you? Who are the women-goddesses who inspirit your life by reminding you of your divine feminine birthright to live blissfully and love freely? Your inspiration or role model may be your mother, your best friend, or your grandmother. She may be embodied in your mind as Jacqueline Kennedy Onassis, once described as a woman of "quintessential intelligence, unremitting elegance, uncommon beauty, relentless poise, and true class." Perhaps you feel the essence of the goddess in a woman who is physically vibrant like Princess Diana in her prime, spiritually resonant like Mother Teresa, or shines energetically like Tina Turner. Maybe you envision a full-spirited woman like Kate Winslet or a lighthearted and playful Goldie Hawn. She may be a three-year-old child, an acquaintance, the old woman with the beautiful smile, or a very personal image—like Glinda—that you have held close to your heart throughout your life.

The Goddess Coronation

Make a list of the fascinating women (from the past or present) whom you admire and respect; it can be anyone you feel a connection with. Focus on the most outstanding and endearing trait of each that would give her "goddess status" in your mind. Next to her name, decree her "goddess of _____." For instance,

Glinda, the goddess of serenity;

Mom, goddess of optimism;
and so on. Lavish admiration on your muses.

Now, identify your finest quality.

Proclaim yourself goddess of _____.
Write it down and share your gift with the world!

A woman who opens her life to the goddess also honors the goddess within herself. It is vital to choose your muse and enrich your love with the strength drawn from the intimate liaison with your cosmic mentor. From the beginning of time, she has appeared in our psyches as a trinity of female splendor and mystery—maiden-muse, madonna-mistress, wisewoman-witch. Her purpose is unmistakable—to encourage you and counsel you in matters of the heart.

Call on the goddess—the muse, the mother, the mistress, the mentor—for guidance, strength, and inspiration. Draw on love's natural cycles as reflected in the primal laws of the Earth and universe, not in the scriptures of man and mortals. Open your hearts with faith and courage, and *know* that the natural phases of love—the Vision, the Enchantment, the Passion, the Celebration—are sustained and empowered by the light of the moon, the replenishing energy of the sun, and the steadfastness of the Earth. Within this enriched embrace of the goddess, claim your radiance, honor your vision, free your dreams, and rewrite the book of love from your own heart's perspective.

There's a New Light in Your Eyes

Who told you that true love is a serious, heavy, "until death do us part" obligatory affair? Who said that the adrenalin-laced romance of new love never lasts, that this bliss is a side-effect of a temporary hormonal and chemical imbalance in "starry-eyed" lovers? And for that matter, what is wrong with being starry-eyed? Who told you these things? If you cannot point your finger to any valid source, then when did the rumors spread like wildfire and why has love gotten such a touchy reputation?

Mortals. All of them. Mortals believe these things and mortals tell you these things. Mortal decrees with their relentless "good girl, bad girl" judgments have ruffled your spirit with these tales. *Love.* So many hearts fear it; so many souls doubt it; and so many lovers wash up drowned in a muck of guilt and obligation. And most likely, because you are weary of relationship roulette or defending your ideals, you've taken some of these mortal opinions to heart and have subscribed to the goddessless tough-love newsletter.

Until today. From this moment into eternity, you will honor love for the tender, fortifying, and refreshing gift that it has always been. After you close this book, love will sneak up on you and astound you with revitalized esprit. So cancel your subscription to the past; you are going to rewrite the "book of love" from your own personal, completely authentic perspective.

Are you ready? I invite you to embrace this collective effervescence of the goddess' spirit and let love flow through your body like a river of pleasure. Be a prism through which the radiant light of love in the universe shimmers, casting rainbow upon rainbow of promise, hope, and vision. *You are a goddess in love.* From virginity to eternity, you can choose to illuminate your days—and nights—with a resistless and divine luminescent love filled with zeal, joy, and peace. Now, follow the *golden*-brick road. . . .

It's always best to start at the beginning.
—GLINDA, the Good Witch of the North, *The Wizard of Oz*

CHAPTER 2

The Vision

The Light of Winter's Wisdom

The Light of Winter's Wisdom

Nature's cycles are woman's cycles. . . .
She does not have to become *but only to* be.
—CAMILLE PAGLIA

The wish is yours. A zillion stars adorn the midnight sky on a clear, crisp winter night. The earth beneath you is still, robust with the beauty of the present and expectant with the promise of the future. 'Tis the season to hold your dreams firmly against your heart and enrich them with the power of your hopes as they germinate and grow. Choose your star, kiss the sky, and make your wish!

If living a life rich with love is your desire, ignite your goddess power *now,* when the universe is most receptive to your petition. Your intuition flows most potently at the new moon, while Mother Earth, this season's elemental "guardian of the watchtower," lends a secure foundation for planning, sorting feelings, resting, and preparing for your passage into awareness. During this gestation between endings and beginnings, the moon—our great lunar lady—is at her newest, so also her darkest, glory. Because of this, no confusing shadows will be cast on your intentions. The goddess will help you delve into the dark lunar aspects of your subconscious and illuminate the wisdom, self-knowledge, and self-love resting there. The gift of this solstitial season is *vision*—light returns to open your heart and you see love reborn.

The intrinsic cycles of love, like the phases of the moon, transcend imperfection simply by *being:* the moon is never too bright, the weather is never too stormy, the sky is never too beautiful, fire is never too hot, water too moist, nor the wind too breezy. Likewise, love is never too perplexing nor too fleeting. It simply is as it is.

As writer Anaïs Nin suggested, you see things not as *they* are, you see them as *you* are. If you lack a clear vision of love, it will elude you—it is that simple. When you talk about it too much—wanting it, having it, lacking it, looking for it—love becomes limited, conditional, and objectified. In its need to be enveloped in mystery, love will retreat, and become as silent as the night in winter.

But within the dark circle of winter's silence, mystery exists. Here love is indefinable, unutterable. And naturally, this is as it should be. For during this symbolic season of purified love, it is a time to glide through the looking glass, clarify the optical illusions of your mind's notion of romantic love, and see the gifts of winter's pristine, though often unyielding, reality. It is a time to be resolutely honest with yourself as you envision and ascertain what you want in love—and most importantly, what you are capable of giving. You have entered love's realm of winter, planted deeply within a zone of regeneration, purification, and blunt realization. It is a time to reflect, recharge, and rededicate your intentions.

Explore and examine your own personal *law of love*. For millennia, the divine feminine psyche—the spirit of love—has been forced into the shadows by religious dictates ("Sex is bad outside of marriage"), patriarchal fear ("It's witchcraft!"), and women who bought this male-scripted package and chose to subvert their intuitive and healing powers. "Dragged into someone else's rhythm, someone else's dance" for centuries and generations, many of us have lost the connection with our goddess-spirit—and often ourselves and our truest beliefs—and remain subservient still to avoid conflict, punishment, or being burned at society's proverbial stake.

The homecoming call to search deeply within your heart and rekindle your goddess light can elicit profound fear and denial. Just remember, you are never required to renounce that which fills you with hope, love, and faith, including your relationship with "God the father," the inspiring philosophies of your comforting religion, or the man who loves you. I only encourage you to unburden your mind, open your heart, and "take the best and leave the rest." And in the quietest corner of your soul, you know what that is.

Love Is Born

*T*raditionally, the Yule festival of the winter solstice, on or near December 21, which finds its genesis in the ancient goddess-earth societies, celebrates the birth of light from the dark womb of the universe. From the solstice forward, the world grows in ever-increasing light. The goddess is also reborn at this time of the year, when Persephone leaves the confines of her consort and begins her journey back from the shadows to share her supernal feminine power.

In mid-December, Sophia, the Gnostic goddess of wisdom born of the primordial female power *Sige* (silence), emerges into the light of consciousness. Mother Night joins in the celebration and gives birth to light in the darkest hours of December 20, a night when dreams foretell the future. In the more familiar patriarchal Christian tradition, the infant Christ, a personification of love (and the power of love to act as savior), is received by the Earth on December 25 through the embodiment of the Virgin goddess mother, Mary. At the winter solstice the goddess renews herself like Diana by the sacred pool.

In this season of birth and mirth, the goddess turns on her luscious love-light, and naturally your desire to feel loved and cherished is ignited by it. Sing "Joy to the world for love has come!" Whether you are "self-blessed," a woman who is currently alone and unattached to a lover, perhaps attracting and man-ifesting true love in her life, "attention-blessed," a woman enjoying several relationships, or "pledge-blessed" and currently in a committed relationship—engaged, "going steady," married, or are "best friends having great sex" with someone—this is a season that supports clearing, seeing, and realizing what you want in love.

> *Upon my bed at night*
> *I sought him whom my soul loves. . . .*
> —Song of Songs, 3:1

The Soulmate Spell

If you want to attract your soulmate, or bring out the best aspects of your current lover (or lovers), you must have a clear vision of what you deeply admire and/or require. There are surely qualities in a lover that you find attractive and endearing (just as there are traits you find repul-sive, but that is not a goddess' focus). But perhaps you haven't s-l-o-w-e-d down and paused, to be alone with your feelings, to confront your true desires, envision a life rich with love, and be grateful for what you already have attracted. So you find yourself on the brink of ennui or on boring dates with Mr. Not-Quite-Right when you could be holding Mr. Fantasy in your arms. The time is ripe to do the Soulmate Spell. (This also works for encouraging Mr. Almost Right to transform himself into *Mr. Perfectly Fine.*)

While feasting on a freshly baked batch of *Midwinter Springerle* (recipe follows) to enhance your senses, clothe yourself in something white and comfortable and light a red candle with the words *soulmate, dream man,* or something similar on it. Pour yourself a refreshment—a glass of spirits, water, or a cup of cardamom tea.

On a sheet of virgin parchment paper begin your list, using a pen with purple ink. Write it in the present tense and phrase your desires in a positive sense (do not scrawl, "He doesn't do this or won't do that"—the goddess does not understand negative concepts, and you must avoid creating by "default").

Open your soul and let it flow: "He loves to swim naked in the ocean at night. . . . He is a great kisser. . . . He laughs at himself and knows the definition of humor. . . . He is faithful. . . . He has a healthy and natural body with nice shoulders. . . . He is free to love. . . . He speaks at least ten words of another language. . . . He respect elders and children. . . . He loves his mom. . . . He believes in financial abundance. . . . He is a savvy traveler. . . . He is brave enough to make love to me at night in a haunted castle during a thunderstorm. . . ."

Write everything down that is true for you. Then fold your list, by turning the top of the paper over and *toward* you, then turn it clockwise and fold it again, and turn and fold one more time. Anoint it with anise or cinnamon oil, kiss the list, and put it where sunlight and moonlight can energize it. Say aloud, *"So it shall be—or better!"* Now set your sights on your soulmate and get out of the goddess' way!

The Magic in Your Hands

There's an old belief that claims if you want to attract a lover or fortify the love you have, create something with your own hands to be given as a gift. Through this act, you weave your energy, talents, and desires into the very essence of your creation, which will release a bewitching spell when you bestow it upon your love-interest.

Allow your imagination to help you create something unique and appealing. Write a poem on handmade paper, sew a poet's shirt, or paint a self-portrait. Plant a shamrock in a custom-made ceramic pot, make a bookmark by laminating a four-leaf clover, or embroider a silk cloth.

When I was a wild, "attention-blessed" goddess, I would knit an afghan for each of my suitors. I stopped knitting, however, after losing a man I truly cherished for whom I'd made a beautiful Icelandic sweater. I discovered, all too late, an Italian superstition that holds if you knit a sweater for a lover, he'll wear it when he walks away. So be wise and study your spells before you begin.

A Perfect Token of Good Taste

Lore has it that Springerle, traditional Germanic cookies, carried the impression of an animal so they could be offered as tokens of worship to hungry pagan deities in place of more expensive live animal sacrifices. Some were stamped with the imprint of the evergreen, a sacred tree of immortality honored at the winter solstice. As with many pagan offerings, *Springerle* were swept up in the resourceful Christian practice of transforming mysterious Yule party fare into safer Christmas cheer. Now *Springerle* are imprinted with Christmas trees and cute little reindeer. The cookie still possesses a touch of magic, which is evident in its taste. With a prized batch of these as your contribution to the love goddesses presiding at winter solstice, your requests will be granted.

Midwinter Springerle

1 cup butter

2 cups white sugar

2 eggs

1 tablespoon finely grated lemon zest

1 tablespoon orange zest, optional

5 teaspoons anise extract

4 cups unbleached flour

2 teaspoons baking powder

2 teaspoons milk

Extra sugar to sprinkle on cookies

Cream the butter and sugar together and beat in eggs until fluffy. Add the citrus zest and the anise extract and mix together gently. Mix the baking powder into the flour and gradually tap this mixture into the creamed ingredients. Dribble milk around the edges of the bowl and mix until a soft dough forms.

Divide the dough into two pieces to make it easy to work with. On a floured surface, roll the dough out to a ¼-inch thickness. Use your *Springerle* mold to make impressions or cut shapes with a favorite cookie cutter. Place cookies on a parchment-lined baking sheet and lightly sprinkle the tops with sugar.

To honor the tradition of letting the cookies charge their charms, cover the molded, unbaked cookies with a towel and let them rest overnight or for up to 8 hours. (You also have the choice to bake them right away if you prefer.)

Preheat oven to 325° F. Bake for 12 to 15 minutes or until the cookies begin to crack on top or take on a hint of color. Cool and store in an airtight tin. Makes 4 dozen 1-inch cookies.

Plant a wishing tree. In magical days of yore, trees were thought to house indwelling spirits that would aid those who evoked their powers. Certain trees are especially potent for invoking the forces of love: the apple tree for spells, divination, and healing; the cherry tree for magic and romance; the oak for stamina, lust, and fertility; and the willow and peach trees for love magic and healing the heart.

When visiting the tree, hang a token such as a crystal, ribbon, or charm on its branch, and make your wish. Invite your beloved and close friends to do the same. Then randomly choose a token to take with you. Though the charm you hang holds the power of your wish, it is only when someone unties it and takes it that the energy of your intention is released and your wish will be fulfilled.

Candle Color Magic

Fire has been sacred since it was discovered, and the candle has become the quintessential emblem of this element's power. The flame's ability to transform, purify, and fortify has been revered by every culture on earth. No goddess would be without her candles.

To engage in purposeful candlework, you should take great care to use the appropriate color of candle, dress or anoint the candle fittingly, and properly dispose of the candle's remnants. To dress the candle, stroke it from the center upward and the center downward with the chosen empowering oil or "holy water." You may also etch the name of the person you are "working on" or the intention of your candle on its side or bottom. Candles must be properly grounded in sturdy and secure candlesticks or votive glasses to ensure safety while burning. Always cleanse the candle holder in sea salt and water before burning a new candle in it; salt dispels residual energies from prior burnings. To dispose of candle remains, I suggest that you bury them away from your house or discard in a public garbage container.

Most importantly, don't discuss your candle magic with others; it will dilute your intention. As Julia Cameron counsels, "The first rule of magic is self-containment. You must hold your intention within yourself, stoking it with power. Only then will you be able to manifest what you desire."

Color Attribute

Red	Love, passion, courage, charisma, invoking divine spirit.
Orange	Concentration, healthy sexuality, emotional stability.
Yellow	Attraction and creativity.
Green	Abundance, health, positive flow of money, stability.
Sky Blue	Intuition, peace.
Indigo	Protection, clairvoyance, supernal vision.
Purple	Power, divine power channeled from God/dess.

White	Purification, blessing, clarity.
Pink	Honor, friendship, gaiety.
Silver	Serenity, moon meditation.
Gold	Ultimate wealth of spirit, dreams come true.
Black	Release.

Goddesses of Light

This is the season to invoke the goddess of light. The passionately adored Sophia (symbolized by the Dove of Aphrodite, from which the emblem of the Holy Ghost was mirrored) represents God's female soul and source of his power as the Virgin of Light in time of darkness. Isis, the exalted Egyptian goddess of creation, appears with a message of great love for her consort Osiris. But she also teaches that love is a dance—you draw near, connect with romance and sexual passion, then pull away, and finally reunite with the ability to maintain the bond of love even through death.

Unaffected by the dictates of any mortal or god, Athena with "the flashing eyes" appears to offer the gifts of undiluted strength, wisdom, and the affirmation of free will. The divine huntress Diana inspires you to take charge of your body and life with her wildness and connection to nature as she commands the all-encompassing power of her beloved moon.

In this season of wisdom, the shadow goddess Persephone shares her promise of renewal and enduring love by confronting the darker side of life.

Beautiful and nonchalant, this "radiant and luminous playmate of the Seasons" was only concerned with meadow breezes and the dalliances of nature when she was abducted and torn away from her mother's love. Yet by accepting her role as queen consort in the world of eternal night, Persephone triumphed over the fear and doubt of separation. Though her love is quiet and reserved during the winter months, she returns each spring to the comfort of her meadows and the eternal love of Demeter, her Mother Nature.

Just as you begin to feel a change in the days and hear the echo of a new season, Juno Februa, patroness of February, the "love month," awakens you with her signature trait: *febris,* the fever of love. She introduces herself as she truly is—the original Valentine. And then there's Brigid, the bright goddess who holds the torch from which you ignite your lovelight, who arrives at Candlemas on February 2 to purify your heart and make all things new again.

> *How many cares one loses when one decides not*
> *to be something but to be someone.*
> —COCO CHANEL

Hold a Candle to Love

*A*mong Celtic pagans, Candlemas was observed in the sacred calendar as a fire festival called Imbolc, which heralded the increasing warmth of the days and the subsequent fertility of those days (and nights). In ancient Rome, this day was sacred to the lascivious Juno Februa, goddess of passionate love and mother of Mars, who was worshiped by lovers carrying candles, symbolic of their newly-lit sexual fires.

Christians, of course, capitalized on the purifying aspect of the flame and rededicated Candlemas as the "Feast of the Purification of the Virgin," which was based on the notion that a woman must be "purified" for forty days after giving birth. (Speaking of flames, the Virgin Mary was said to have conceived by being "fecundated by the sacred fire"—*igne sacro inflammata.*) Regardless of why and for whom the fires burn, love is still love, sex is still sex, and Candlemas celebrates the intrigue of both.

Secrets of a Good-Time Goddess

*A*nother darling at February's fiery love party is the frisky Celtic Earth goddess Brigid (a.k.a. Saint Brigit, Ireland's lively patroness who was known for her miraculous ability to change bathwater into beer to refresh thirsty priests). Venerated initially as the fertility goddess and mystical poetess Brigid to her pagan fans, and later as the feisty (her name literally means "fiery arrow") and fervent Saint Brigit to her Christian admirers, this inspiring, multifaceted soul sister has held high court in the hearts of her faithful for centuries.

Her favors were invoked to keep life's mantle warm and the promise of everlasting love protected. Brigid was especially fond of poets and writers, healers, and smiths, and could be called upon by her cult—when important inside information was necessary—to illuminate the mind with her power of augury. To secure her blessings for love and fertility, worshipers would offer the likely forerunners of modern-day cinnamon rolls: special spicy buns made with honey.

Delighting in the images of the goddess Brigid and her buns (and what we know about the aphrodisiac aspects of cinnamon), I offer you this magical recipe to appease the Goddess of the Lovelight—and the lucky recipient of that light.

Brigid's Cinnamon Buns

The Dough

    ¹⁄₂ cup sugar (or ¹⁄₃ cup honey)

    ¹⁄₂ cup rolled oats

    1¹⁄₂ cups buttermilk, warmed

    ¹⁄₄ cup lukewarm water

    1 tablespoon SAF-Instant yeast

    2 eggs

    ¹⁄₄ cup canola oil

    1 teaspoon salt

    1 teaspoon ground cinnamon

    ¹⁄₂ teaspoon ground cardamom

    6 to 6¹⁄₂ cups unbleached flour

Filling

> 2 cups white or raw sugar
>
> 1³⁄₄ cups brown sugar
>
> ¹⁄₄ cup ground cinnamon
>
> 1 teaspoon ground nutmeg
>
> 1 cup raisins
>
> 1 tablespoon rum
>
> ¹⁄₂ cup melted butter
>
> 1 cup chopped pecans

Glaze

> 2 cups powdered sugar
>
> 3 tablespoons milk (or 1 tablespoon orange juice plus 2 tablespoons milk)

First make the dough. In a large bowl, combine sugar (or honey) and oats, and pour warm buttermilk over it. Stir and set aside for 5 minutes. In another very large ceramic "bread" bowl, add water and sprinkle the yeast over it. Let rest for a few minutes. Then add eggs, oil, salt, spices, and 2 cups flour. Mix together. Add buttermilk mixture to the flour mixture, stirring steadily. Gradually add the remaining flour and form a soft, not-too-sticky dough.

Knead on a well-floured surface for 4 to 6 minutes. Place in a greased bowl, cover, and set aside in a warm area until double in size (about 30 minutes if you use SAF-Instant yeast).

To make the filling, blend the sugars and spices together. Soak the raisins in rum. Prepare a large baking pan (a 16 x 11 x 2¼-inch lasagne-size pan works best; two 9-inch round pans will work, too) by brushing the bottom with some of the butter and sprinkling ½ to ¾ cup of the sugar mix on the bottom of the pan. Reserve the rest of the sugar mixture and the butter.

Without punching the dough down, shape it and roll it into a large rectangle on a well-floured surface. Fold the rectangle lengthwise into thirds—"shorter" edges toward the center, like folding a letter—and roll out again into a ¼-inch thick, 12 x 18-inch rectangle. Brush the dough with melted butter and sprinkle the sugar mixture evenly over the dough, followed by the raisins and nuts. Starting with the longer side, roll the dough—not too tightly—toward you, "jelly-roll" style.

Using a very sharp knife, cut the dough into 1¼-inch thick slices and place them in the prepared pan spiral side up. Tuck the "tail" of the dough under the bun. Cover and let rest until doubled in size (another 30 minutes).

Preheat oven to 350° F. Bake for 25 minutes or until the rolls are a radiant golden brown. While baking, make the glaze by combining ingredients in a small bowl. When hot out of the oven, slather the buns with glaze and indulge! Makes a baker's dozen deluxe buns.

Brigid's Tips

- SAF-Instant yeast can be purchase through King Arthur Flour Company, 800-827-6836. However, if you are using regular yeast in place of SAF-Instant yeast, then follow this procedure: In a small separate bowl, dissolve a pinch of sugar in ¼ cup warm water; sprinkle the yeast on top and set aside. Add the yeast solution to the dough after mixing in the initial 2 cups of flour. Rising time will take longer with dry active yeast; the dough is ready when it has doubled. Note time for the future.

- For romantic breakfasts in bed without the hassle of all the "bun-building," prepare the buns ahead of time. After placing rolls in the pan, cover them—uncooked and unproofed—with plastic and refrigerate for up to 12 hours. Before baking, remove the plastic, cover the buns with a clean towel dampened with hot water, let rise, and bake in a preheated oven.

- Baked, unglazed buns will keep in an airtight container for a day or two. If you wish to freeze the buns, store them sticky-side-up in a lined pan covered with foil and plastic. To reheat, either remove plastic and bake in foil at 375° F for 15 minutes, or microwave on HIGH, uncovered on a plate, for 30 seconds. Lather with fresh glaze and serve warm.

A woman who doesn't wear perfume has no future.
—COCO CHANEL

When we refer to the "sweet smell of romance," we may no longer be merely alluding to a metaphorical state of bliss and arousal, but to a biochemical one. In humankind's almost comical obsession to discover and employ aphrodisiacs, we've purloined bags of M&M's to harvest the green ones, rolled around in silk sheets, and spent fortunes on designer perfumes. Even vegetables and nuts have reputed aphrodisiac qualities—remember, Popeye claimed spinach made him "good to the finich" and Dr. Ruth swears she's had success with chestnut puree. Now research seems to be telling us, "Drop everything and go bake a batch of cinnamon rolls."

In one study, the penile bloodflow of thirty-one male medical students was measured when subjects whiffed a range of fragrances from perfume to suntan oil to roses to black licorice. Every odor boosted the flow from one intensity to another, but some fragrances hit the jackpot, so to speak. Among the super-erotic turn-ons were the aromas of pumpkin pie, lavender, and doughnuts. The seductress of all fragrances, however, proved to be that of the sexy, spice-laced cinnamon roll!

Lunar Love Lights

*The well-instructed moon flies not from her orbit
to seize on the glories of her partner.*
—MARGARET FULLER, *THE DIAL*

In addition to embracing the seasons of love, a woman living in the light of the goddess wisely attunes her life with the cycles of Mother Nature's jewel, the moon. Each phase of the moon possesses a distinct alchemical allure. And this power is very real. Imagine having the ability to command the tides to recede or the birds and beasts to migrate.

Consider the greatest force of all—woman's power to create life. This astonishing process is inseparable from the cyclical force of the moon's rays: our life is reflected in hers as we share 28½ days of creating, attracting, climax, and release. Women who are holistically attuned to the moon's feminine spirit will often menstruate when the moon is new and ovulate when she is full.

In matters of body and soul, turn to the moon for guidance. Remember, it is of paramount importance that you consider the phase of the moon as you energize your intentions and call on her natural power; the waxing moon inspires creation and beginnings, the waning moon evokes release and completion.

New Moon. Powerful and quiet night of reflection and rededication; a night to offer the New Moon Meditation and to honor your desires. Though she will remain unseen on this night, look for her newest crescent smile in the southwest corner of the next early evening sky.

Waxing Maiden Moon. Supercharged time of magic, fertility, and growth; a positive time for emanating energy of attraction, manifestation, and creation; begin new projects. Her path follows the sunset later in the evening as she grows.

Full Moon. The night to surrender to the passion of life and love; celebrate the fruits of your intentions; be aware of the illusions cast by the moon's silvery light; don't *try* to be—just *be*. Look to the east after sunset for her to rise, wild and bright.

Waning Sage Moon. Time to emit energy of release; cast spells for diminishing, decreasing, and dissipating; "let go and flow." She is a flighty mistress now, but will appear late at night and in the earliest hours of the morning.

Above all, hold the power of the moon—the very essence of the goddess herself—close to your body and your spirit as you invoke your love magic. Allow her luster to filter into yours, igniting your passion and guiding you toward luminescence—love of yourself, of others, and of life.

New Moon Meditation

*T*he night before every new moon, I draw up a therapeutic, detoxifying mudbath made of moor extracts and a Sylvestri grade of pine essential oil (my favorite is made by Golden Moor, 800-236-7668). While bathing in the candlelight of properly blessed white candles for clarity and purification (see Candle Color Magic, page 25), I breathe in the healing scent of the pine and exhale the unresolved issues in my heart. As I massage my skin with a special dark purple (for power) washcloth that I reserve for this night, I focus on loving and healing myself—body, soul, and mind—and allow the moor mud to extract the impurities and stress from my body. When I am finished, my problems simply go down the drain. I then thoroughly cleanse the tub with sea salt.

On the new moon, I bask in a cleansing bath of sea salts, milk, mint, and luxurious bubbles. I focus on the love flowing in my life and open my heart to the evocative epiphanies flashing about my thoughts and dreams. After I bathe, I invoke the New Moon Meditation, which can be written privately in your journal or on a piece of paper kept in your Goddess Box (see page 135). I keep my answers simple and my goals attainable:

What do I want to release from my life?
What do I wish to manifest?
What am I thankful for?

After the meditation, I honor my goddess muse and complete my invocation by saying aloud: *"So it shall be—or better."* And I always smile because I know that at this moment, a profoundly feminine force in the universe has appeared with the sole purpose to help me manifest what my spirit desires.

Love by the Light of the Moon

*A*s the moon transits through the zodiac during her monthly travels, her influence on the moods, impulses, and desires of the lovers she shines upon becomes obvious to the goddess who attunes herself to lunar law. In astrology, the moon governs emotions, instincts, and the unconscious—the "reactionary" aspects of an individual. Therefore, when planning, playing, and loving, it is wise to stay in tune with the moon.

Knowing someone's "moon sign" will also lend insight to the wild side of their nature; those natural, primitive, sensual urges untamed by conditioning and societal decrees. A good almanac or lunar calendar, such as the *Celestial Pocket Calendar*, and a comprehensive book on astrology (I've listed my favorites at the end of Chapter Six) are indispensable on a goddess' book shelf.

Moon Signs

Moon in Aries. Love is frisky and energized, often impulsive. You are open to change, idealistic, and ready for anything exciting; there is a tendency to be impatient and a little vain.

Moon in Taurus. This is an affectionate time of leisure, trust, and feelings of abundance; it feels good to be home in someone's arms. Beware of being too stubborn or rigid with others.

Moon in Gemini. Communication, quick wit, and changeability are the themes now; you can be very charming and versatile, but you can also be disorganized, superficial, and manipulative; be careful and avoid confusion.

Moon in Cancer. This is a sensitive time; moods can range from being imaginative, creative, and insightful to being possessive, critical, and on the crabby side; you feel best when you're at home.

Moon in Leo. "See and be seen" is the calling during this period of colorful, creative, broad-minded fun. Of course, during all the partying you may seem self-indulgent or overbearing and romantic to a fault.

Moon in Virgo. When you feel the urge to clean the house, pay the bills, and return all unanswered phone calls, the moon is in Virgo. Though it feels natural to be critical and argumentative, try to listen and lighten up.

Moon in Libra. Beauty and balance, charm and diplomacy, and the desire to make love and talk more highlight this time. If you feel neglected, however, you become dependent, self-indulgent, and react frivolously.

Moon in Scorpio. Your need for privacy and sex are intensified by a very emotional and determined imagination as psychic abilities are enhanced. Do you feel jealous, secretive, or resentful? Ask yourself, "Why?"

Moon in Sagittarius. The moon sparkles with adaptability, optimism, exuberance, lightheartedness, and a grand sense of adventure. In love, however, this often translates into restlessness and disinterest in commitment.

Moon in Capricorn. You may feel more determined, focused, and committed during this time of healing and fertility. Stay in tune with your intuition to avoid being ultramaterialistic, opinionated, and pessimistic.

Moon in Aquarius. Your approach to love reaches uncanny heights of idealism, creativity, and tolerance. This may be mistaken for unpredictable aloofness—i.e., spaciness—so try to stay aware and somewhat grounded.

Moon in Pisces. This is a sensitive, loving, romantic time of creativity and intense feelings of loyalty. Your vulnerability may tempt you to resort to secrecy or vagueness if you feel discontented or confused. Let it flow.

Aromas of the Soul

She was so perfumed that the winds were lovesick.
—SHAKESPEARE, *ANTHONY AND CLEOPATRA*

The sense of smell is said to invoke the ancient memories of our souls. You are probably aware of the perfume you sprayed on your wrists this morning or the aroma of a pine-scented candle burning at your desk. But it is the more subtle, often undetectable, atavistic scents such as sexual pheromones, the individual scent of your mate, or the faintest fragrance of jasmine on a gentle breeze that incite your body and spirit to respond to love.

Aromatherapists have known these secrets for centuries, and goddesses have been quick to claim the powers of special essential aromas as their own. Learning the sensual codes to the ancient art of aromatherapy and applying it resourcefully with the beguiling skills of your imagination is clearly a talent of an aspiring goddess in love.

To fortify your vision in love, infuse your senses with pine essential oil, which clears negativity, raises determination, and increases the power of the will. Cedarwood and mandarin possess calming and soothing qualities and also aid in purifying, grounding, and clearing confusion. The magical properties of bay include the ability to enhance insight, clarity, awareness, and peace as the presence of its aroma dispels confusion. Mint and anise encourage optimism and attract visions; cardamom clears the mind and uplifts the spirit.

By the way, let it be known that Cleopatra's secret to seduction was in her perfume, a custom blend of rose, cardamom, and cinnamon oil. She always wore this enticing scent when meeting with Marc Anthony "to awaken and kindle to fury passions that as yet lay still and dormant in his nature." Perhaps she should have added a drop of bay for a little more wisdom—or applied some other aromatic unguent to repel the kiss of the asp.

Aromatherapy's Essential Arts

For aromatherapy to be effective and ultimately enjoyable, utilize the full spectrum of indulgences in their various applications. When anointing your senses with essential oils, it is often important to blend them with a base substance before applying them directly to the skin (some, like cinnamon oil, are much too irritating if not diluted). The following recipes offer guidelines for mixing oils for a variety of application methods and uses. Of course, use more or less essential oil as you desire.

Bath	Mix 6 to 10 drops essential oil with 1 tablespoon (½ ounce) of unscented bath oil per full tub of water.

Massage	Add 6 to 10 drops essential oil to a base of 2 tablespoons (1 ounce) unscented grapeseed or sweet almond massage oil.
Perfume	Add 13 drops essential oil to 1 teaspoon (⅙ ounce) jojoba oil for perfume, or 13 drops to 1 tablespoon alcohol for cologne.
Atomizer	Add 6 drops essential oil to every 1 ounce of spring water. Shake before using.
Inhalation	Add 4 to 7 drops essential oil to a large bowl of hot water. Cover head with a towel and breathe deeply for 5 to 7 minutes. Relax.
Diffuser	Add 6 to 10 drops essential oil to 2 table-spoons water or follow specific directions for your type of diffuser.
Facial Oil	Add 6 drops essential oil to 1 tablespoon of facial oil; massage gently. Sweet almond, jojoba, and evening primrose oils work well.
Compress	Mix 6 drops essential oil to every cup of hot or cold water used.

Love Note

⊘ Mist your pillows with an atomizer and remember to put a few drops of a favorite essential oil in the toilet bowl or bidet.

The Goddess Gates of Ecstasy

I remember breezes
from winds inside your body. . . .
—DONNA GODCHAUX, "SUNRISE"

*A*ncient Tantric wisdom, a Hindu/Buddhist yogic tradition that seeks the "ineffable bliss of divine union" through mystical sexual practices, teaches that there are seven subtle energy centers in the body through which the life force flows. These "wheels of ecstasy" are called *chakras*, a Sanskrit word meaning "wheel" or "disc." Each chakra acts as an invisible energy vortex that emits a specific vibration and emanates a certain color in the "aura" of an individual.

An activated chakra acts as a "psychic relay station" that sends energy from person to person or from the subconscious to the conscious mind. In Tantra, the chakras are also honored as secret centers through which the ultimate orgasmic union with the divine is achieved. A goddess in the know keeps her gates—and her lover's—open and clear and the energy whirling through them.

In love's season of Vision, you will be empowered by focusing on the first root or base chakra—"I am"—and by stabilizing the sixth or Third Eye chakra which asserts, "I see." The root chakra, which vibrates slowly from the base of the spine, glowing with a dark, rich red hue, is the fire in the belly. This goddess gate opens to survival, self-preservation, and the powerful ability to manifest a sense of purpose. To maintain and protect the vitality of the physical body, it is essential that this chakra is balanced by proper diet, visualization, therapeutic bathing, and relaxation. (I am an avid believer in the chakra-balancing exercises and diet outlined by Sonia Choquette in *The Psychic Pathway*.)

When the Third Eye chakra is open and balanced, you are intuitive, creative, and aware of the those little voices in your soul. This is the visionary's gate of altruism, inner peace, perception, and ultimate truth. As the chakra whirrs in the center of your forehead, a deep shade of indigo blue emanates from its center. Here you have the ability to perceive love and to "see" your dreams come true. Place your middle and ring fingers on your third eye and begin massaging this center in a counterclockwise direction—open your goddess gate of vision *now*.

Believe and Receive

*N*ow as I watch rerun after rerun of *The Wizard of Oz* with my enchanted, wide-eyed daughter at my side, I wonder what kind of advice Glinda would give about love—"finding" love, "falling" in love, and "staying" in love. Her advice would be surely be lucid like her spirit: "You don't need to look any longer; you've always had the power to attract the love you dream of. You simply have to believe it for yourself. Now close your eyes, tap your heels together three times, and repeat. . . ."

I agree with Glinda. You don't need to "find" something that was never really "lost." For so many, the so-called "search for love" is a distraction from the truth that first you must be *able* to love. And to do this, you have to gather up the strength of all your dreams and experiences, believe in yourself, and reclaim your goddess-given power. The goddess' law of love asserts, *"As you think and are, so you attract."* As you begin to focus and create a life of peace, playfulness, and wonder, you will also attract a pure and natural love.

With a renewed confidence in your heart and your lovelight shining freely and brightly, you will learn to make choices in love that are securely grounded in your love for yourself and the power of your goddess within. Remember, *the secret to loving is loving.* If you tell yourself this at least thirteen times a day, you will experience a beautiful and profound change in your life. It is your birthright and privilege to flourish, grow, and flow with the love of your dreams. A new day is breaking and the promise of love's Enchantment is being ushered in on a delicious spring breeze. Come . . . *laissez les bons temps rouler!*

It's hard to believe unless you believe, but once you believe, it's easy.
—ANONYMOUS

Words of Vision

Your Heart's Desire by Sonia Choquette
Finding True Love by Daphne Rose Kingma
A Woman's Worth by Marianne Williamson
I Had It All the Time by Alan Cohen
To Love and Be Loved by Sam Keen
Illusions by Richard Bach
Succulent Wild Woman by Sark

Love Tips

🌀 Activate the "attraction action" in your life. List three ideas or activities that would complement the Vision of love in your life. Perhaps you have the desire to enhance your physical vibrancy by eating healthful, natural foods or to transform your listless "work-out" at the gym into a vitalizing "play-out"—become comfortably skilled in a new, fun mode of recreation you can enjoy solo or with your lover or with friends, such as horseback riding, hiking for pleasure, or tennis. You may want to tickle your talents by learning a new language or taking a cooking class and mastering the art of sushi-making. If you have never meditated, now is the time. Set three goals and accomplish them, *for fun.*

🌀 Purchase or create a beautiful, luxurious article of clothing in which to meditate, dream, perform your spells, or write in your journal. It should be woven of rich, natural fabric and be predominately white with accents of green, gold, or purple. Think of it as your "goddess garb" and wear it wisely. (The word *clothing* comes from *Clotho*, one of three Fates, who was responsible for spinning the thread of human life and the wild webs of fate in which mortals would ensnare themselves by their desires.)

♀ There couldn't be a better time to give yourself a copy of my book *Goddess in the Kitchen* so you can begin fine-tuning your skills in the timeless art of practical seduction— cooking! Entice *yourself* with the "self-love potions" sprinkled throughout the chapter entitled "Vestal Pleasures: Food for Savoring Solitude." Prepare a feast for yourself! Then move on to "In Aphrodite's Mixing Bowl," where you will learn everything you need to know about being a spell-mixing kitchen courtesan. (With these recipes as your guide, I *promise* you satisfaction in love.)

♀ Enhance your life with the colors of the season. Decorate your home and yourself in shades of deep, rich green, the color of the evergreen tree, the symbol of eternal life and love. Orange represents the birth of the sun and emergence of light, silver reflects the omnipresent power of the moon, and winter white vibrates to the peace and purity of the heart.

♀ Listen to the music and the lyrics of "The Rose," recorded by Bette Midler.

The Vision of love *enlightens* you.

> *Our first responsibility is to amuse ourselves;*
> *if we can't do that, then we can't entertain anyone.*
> —BOB WEIR

CHAPTER 3

The Enchantment

The Eternal Promise of Spring

The Promise and Sweetness of Spring

What I love is near at hand,
always, in earth and air.
—THEODORE ROETHKE

An ethereal breeze sweeps across the morning dew on the daisies and the air is peaceful and cool. The sunrise glorias of eager birds fill the air and the frog song in the pond swells in crescendo with the warming rays of light. Ahh, listen to the music. . . . Spring has come to seduce you. Aphrodite, the elegant muse of creativity, beauty, and love giggles and dances with Aurora, goddess of the dawn and sister of the moon, and Oshun, mistress of the crescent moon and the "daughter of promise." Cupid listens to their laughter, arrow drawn.

In this moment of gold, the promise of love is sacred.

Imagine a field of lush, emerald green grass kissed by warm, caressing breezes and blanketed in tiny white wildflowers, violets, daffodils, and daisies. Imagine playing in this field with your beloved—dancing, dreaming, rolling in the grass, running barefoot through the flowers, drinking fruit juice from your consort's cup until the nectar spills and flows slowly down your sun-warmed body. . . . You lie in each other's arms watching the clouds roll by, divining adventures in the wake of their billowy folds. All the goddesses smile.

You are *in love*—the playground of the great goddess. The spring equinox, which arrives around March 20, is the great "festival of freshness," a time when the balance and beauty of love is at its most evocative level. In this season of love, the crescent moon is beginning to swell in the skies, reflecting all your hopes and wishes in her light. Love's tempo is increasing; you notice it in the flush of the sunlight as the days grow longer. In this season of playfulness and wonder, "sweet desire weds wild delight," and you feel a drastic stirring in your soul as your body and mind are strengthened and refreshed. Aphrodite's laughter has heralded the official opening of the mating season.

The "Return of the Goddess," or Lady Day, celebrated each spring on March 25, also holds the honor of being the Feast of the Annunciation, the day when the world is promised divine love in its physical manifestation. In love's circle of Enchantment, Aphrodite and her twin sister Venus hold court as the belles of love's ball. The Yoruba goddess Oshun "perfumes her skin with honey" and decorates herself with flowing scarves of yellow and green, enticing her lover with gifts of bells, oranges, and pastries. Riding through the fields on her great white mare, the enchantress Rhiannon promises fertility and charisma to those who embrace her magic and beauty.

The Divine Timing of Love

ove comes into your life right on time. You can't force it or rush it or command it to appear. Though often cloaked in its many mysterious guises, you must receive love when it arrives; if your heart is not open you can miss it or even sabotage it. Therefore a goddess is always *aware:* just as you notice the growing light of the goddess Luna in the twilight skies and the newest, fuzziest baby buds on the trees along your walk, you are aware when you attract the attentions of a suitor. It is essential at this moment of recognition—your eyes meet, he asks you out for lunch, or you notice he is watching you at the gym—that you reserve all judgment (i.e., what he does, has, or wants) and *relish the moment.*

In the spring of love, be a goddess who flirts, dallies, plays, and allows time for the blossom of enchantment to unfold. Bask in the Enchantment for months, *years* if possible—oh, please never, ever, *ever* rush through this season of love. Fine-tune your most seductive and captivating feminine wiles (keep reading!). Pamper yourself in every way you can afford: clothe yourself in sensual clothing, get massages, release that last bit of unnecessary weight, get or give yourself facials, take long, luxurious baths, and rest well. Every morning when you awake, announce aloud:

I am a radiating center of divine love.
Love is moving through my cells like sunlight through a prism.

Be assured, the goddess is all about you, to inspirit you with her sensual wisdom. Let your feelings flow, freely, naturally, and playfully. Saunter into the embrace of love's mysterious allure, serene and confident—and prepare to ascend in love. . . .

Get on your mark. . . . Keep your vision focused, your heart buoyant, relish the moment, and delight in the sight of your lover;

Get set . . . . Call on your muses, radiate physical vitality, free yourself for fun, relax and breathe;

Go! . . . Be a goddess of Action, Magic, Grace, and Power! Bask in Enchantment!

Just trust yourself, then you will know how to live.
—GOETHE

The Attraction Bath

If your soul is shining a green light to your heart and you honestly are ready to entice someone with your charm, prepare to stir up some action. One of the most potent places for invoking the magnetic power of love is in a bubble-charged bath during a new crescent moon. A specially "dressed" candle creates the symbolic lovelight that will aid in drawing a lover to you while providing the universal elements of fire, air, water, and earth to enhance and fortify your intention.

Essential oils rich in their power of attraction enliven your senses and bring the attentions of the love goddesses—including the wild and wonderful goddess-spirit within you—into focus. The seductive scents include jasmine, rose, lavender, lily of the valley, Roman chamomile, magnolia, and cinnamon. If you are truly prepared, the time has arrived to draw upon your desires and nourish them with the secrets of the Attraction Bath.

- Above all, accept the universal law that you cannot *make* someone fall in love with you. But if someone is intrigued by you, or your purpose is to captivate your current paramour for a night of passion, the law of attraction applies unquestionably. Write the word *love* (and the name of the person you want to "work on" if you have someone in your sights) on a yellow candle. Then anoint the candle with a favorite essential oil, stroking it from the center upward and the center downward. Place it in a candle holder that has been purified with sea salt and water.

• Clean your tub with sea salt and visualize all doubt washing down the drain as you rinse it. Then, prepare your bath with abundant silky bubbles (Ultra Palmolive for sensitive skin creates supreme bubbles) and your favorite bath salts, filling it to the brim with the hottest water you can endure. For this bath, I use "Romancing Rose" Sacred Salts from AuraRoma (800-253-2476) or unscented bath salts to which I add six drops of rose oil and six drops of jasmine oil. Add a capful of Love Oil.

Love Oil

   3 ounces apricot kernel oil
   3 ounces sweet almond oil
   1 ounce (2 tablespoons) aloe vera gel
   ½ ounce rosewater
   13 drops jasmine essential oil
   6 drops rose essential

Blend the apricot kernel oil, sweet almond oil, aloe vera gel, and rosewater together in an 8-ounce bottle. Shake well. Add the jasmine and rose and oils. Shake well before using.

• As you undress, envision yourself kissing the person you desire (please, you must be clear in your intention before proceeding). Toss a handful each of dried yarrow flowers, parsley, and chamomile into the water to steep.

- Light your candle and recite:

> *My heart is open, my spirit is free,*
> *Dear Lady escort my love to me.*
> *So be it, or better.*

- As you bathe (using honey to enhance the power of attraction), bask in the energetic feeling of this love—hear his voice, savor his touch, imagine the moonlight shining in his eyes. If you know his name, insert it into the spell in place of "my love." Call on your imagination to create a circle of enchantment around you as you repeat the words to your petition six times, the number of Venus. As you recite the incantation, you seal the covenant sacred to the law of love. Remain in the bath for a while and read a favorite book of love. Trust that your pledge was heard . . . and then *release the outcome* to the goddess and "surrender to love's high tide." As you get dressed, smile and say "Thank you."

> *The best way to make your dreams*
> *come true is to wake up.*
> —PAUL VALÉRY

*I don't mind the blues in the night,
as long as they're sapphires.*
—LAUREN BACALL

By consciously choosing colors, clothing, or gems to enhance your mood, you are cooperating with the spirit of your inner goddess. My beloved friend, Dorismarie, shared her "Cosmic Color Vibrations" with me long ago, and I enjoy adorning myself with the hues and shades of the day. I also relish the connection of knowing we are vibrating to the same color—goddess to goddess—on any given day regardless of the physical distance that separates us.

Monday	*Blue, iridescent blue, midnight blue;* ruled by the Moon, Selene, and Diana; a day of intuition, self-love, reflection, and love wishes.
Tuesday	*Red or healing pink;* ruled by Mars; from "Tiw's Day"; a day of passion, energy, and truth; "Tuesday is good news day."
Wednesday	*Yellow;* ruled by Mercury; from "Woden's Day"; a day of communication, motivation, mystical resourcefulness, and magic.
Thursday	*Lavender or purple;* ruled by Jupiter; "Thor's Day," also sacred to Oshun; a day of strength,

	spontaneity, stamina, and extravagance.
Friday	*Green;* ruled by Aphrodite/Venus, "Freya's Day"; love, creativity, joyous sexuality, abundance, fertility, and communing with nature.
Saturday	*Black, white, or grey;* ruled by Saturn; a day of practical tasks and accomplishments followed by feasting, revelry, and opulence.
Sunday	*White, orange, or gold;* ruled by the Sun; a day of regeneration, vitality, rest, self-expression, pride, and celebrating life.

The Merry Month of May

In the ancient calendar, and in the goddess' season of Enchantment, May, named for Maia, goddess of spring and rebirth, symbolizes the most joyous time of love and courtship. A collective sense of excitement literally wafts about the breezes as lovers glance and giggle (some say the air sylphs and wood nymphs are out and about casting playful spells on moon-struck lovers). Revelers dance around the frankly phallic Maypoles, which are draped with colorful, flowing ribbons. On Beltane (May Day), a celebration of discovery and sexual enticement, the bonfires burn seductively as impassioned gods chase elusive goddesses about.

Tradition finds you *a-Maying* on May 1, secretly hanging May baskets on doors of those whose attentions you wish to attract. The Roman goddess Flora is always the prettiest girl at the party during her festival of Floralia, marked by lovely bouquets of spring flowers and picnic blankets sprinkled with rose petals. Flowers are everywhere.

The great Norse goddess of beauty and love Freya (also called Frigg), dances in lovers' psyches during this time of readiness and intrigue. When Freya is riding in the heavens in her cat-drawn chariot looking for her beloved consort Od, god of ecstasy, you can look at the stars and see the jewels of her necklace, the Milky Way. Since she knows more magic than the gods, nothing can be lucky without her blessing, especially love. So obvious are her sexual overtures that a common colloquialism for sexual intercourse was named for her dopplegänger, Frigg (use it wisely and respectfully).

Spring represents the "golden moment of love"—a time when your heart feels young, wild, and free. This is the moment you leap and ascend in love, secure in the magnetic attentions of your beloved, and safe in the natural embrace of the world around you. Look around—love's Enchantment is everywhere! The goddesses' holidays in this mellifluous season of the soul remind you that the license to play is infinitely renewable!

Whether you have been with someone for ten days or ten years, you always hold the power to draw on the gift of this season. Love is lighthearted, spirited, and remains unanalyzed now. This is the time to let your lover chase you around the Maypole, regale him with simple gifts, such as a package of Ambrosias (recipe on page 67), hung on his door, and take long evening strolls together under Oshun's maiden moon and Freya's stars.

Venus has her fish and frogs, Diana has her dogs, Freya has her two grey cats, and Rhiannon has her gorgeous, dappled mare. Every goddess has her totem animal; her symbolic liaison between the seen and unseen, the known and the intuited— her cosmic interpreter of the life principle, the soul, the *anima* and *animus*. By observing animal behavior and learning to communicate with a spirit-pet, the great mysteries of love can be unraveled. Many animals teach unconditional love; others teach you to respect wildness and freedom.

There is goddess wisdom in the advice, "If you want to meet someone take a puppy for a walk." After all, "dog" is "god" spelled backwards—these animals do have the power to open hearts and generate happiness. In truth, the mystical powers of a baby, lop-eared bunny cohered my relationship with my now husband-consort. So, open your soul and call your totem home; your animal friend has a gift for you.

Goddess to Goddess: A Word on Pursuit

A goddess never pursues an inattentive lover. She knows her role is simply to attract, choose, and love. If you feel tempted to chase (i.e., convince, coerce, or manipulate for attention) a particular person, he is *not* the lover the universe intended for you. This is not to say you cannot entice a paramour with your wit and beauty, bake him a seductively potent apple pie, or entertain him sumptuously with delightful love letters. But if your intuition (or a goddess friend) is waving a red flag telling you that you are in pursuit, freeze.

Take a deep breath and a cosmic cue from nature—consider the birds and the beasts. It is a rare species on earth where the female resorts to any effort to procure the mating rights of a male (except perhaps the black widow and praying mantis, both of which consume their mates after copulation). Oh, no. Even a female *frog* does not pursue the male frog. So why would *you*, prince potential or no prince potential?

Remember what you learned in grade school. The male of the species is more colorful and physically attractive so that he enjoys an advantage in securing the females' attentions. He must use valuable energy to defend his territory against other potential loverboys, and then display himself, hoping to be chosen. The female's role is to observe these going-ons and choose the male that she desires who exudes the greatest potential as protector and provider (and of course, before another female does so). *Fini.* She has the power of wise and timely choice; he doesn't. He pursues ardently; she does not expend her precious energy on trailing males. This is a divine law of nature, so take heed.

Love is supreme and unconditional; like is nice, but limited.
—DUKE ELLINGTON

The Goddess' Best Beauty Tip

Love is a great beautifier.
—LOUISA MAY ALCOTT, *LITTLE WOMEN*

If you want to enchant your lover with spellbinding radiance and beauty, implore Aurora, goddess of the Dawn, to share her trademark beauty secret: the morning's dew. This spell always works and is especially potent on May Day.

In the early hours of the dawn, seek out a flowerbed, abundant with daisies or jasmine, or a field of lush, finely grown grass and wildflowers (avoid places where fertilizer is used!), all kissed with dew. Kneel near the flowers or grass, facing Aurora's glow in the east. Then, at the very moment her rays of light appear over the horizon, caress your cheeks, lips, nose, and forehead gently with the flowers' petals or blades of grass without using your hands. As you feel the dew anoint your face, say aloud:

Aurora's nectar, radiant dew
Blessed by the morning light so new
As the sun shines in the skies
May my beauty light my lover's eyes.

Your lover will wonder why you look so exceptionally beautiful when he sees you that day. *So it shall be.*

Aphrodite's Lucky Number

From this day into eternity, hedge all your bets on number thirteen. The ancient lunar pagan calendar year is based on the thirteen menstrual cycles of a woman's body "calendar" as reflected by the thirteen cycles of the moon (the Hebrew calendar is also based on moon-worship), giving us thirteen fortunate lunar months of a goddess-graced year.

Of course, because the number thirteen was so sacred to the goddess, early Christian monks were compelled to deem it unlucky in order to convert believers to their new sky god. To the Earth-based societies, Friday the Thirteenth was the luckiest day of all, as it combined the day sacred to the goddesses Freya and Aphrodite with their winning number. In fact, Venus' totem animal, the fish (which is still considered an aphrodisiac because of its association to the goddess of love) was customarily eaten as a fertility charm on Friday. Does any of this sound familiar? Conscientious Catholics still eat fish on Fridays during Lent, but certainly not for fertility. Little do they know, Venus is laughing and cheering them on!

Secrets of an Ecstatician

ust as an esthetician imparts a sensitive philosophy of beauty and artistry on her clients, a skilled *ecstatician* is experienced in the art of bliss and delight. When considering love, you must consider all the senses—sight, touch, scent, hearing, taste. In this season of Enchantment, you artfully activate all the alchemical powers at your fingertips. In the sensuous dance of love, the magnetic qualities of certain tried-and-true scents, such as jasmine, rose, lavender, lily of the valley, chamomile, and magnolia, inspire delicious reactions in a receptive lover. Massage his temples with oils, perfume your clothing and linens, and anoint the steering wheel of his car. He'll keep driving over to your house and really won't know exactly why.

To enhance the effects of spring's Enchantment, wear clothing that is made of the natural colors of the season to seduce the sense of sight: purifying white, empowering violet, attractive lemon yellow, sensual, magical emerald green. A goddess prepares foods rich with Aphrodite's blessing, especially dishes and deserts concocted with her treasured apples, seafood, apricots, peaches, and, of course, *theabroma cacao*, the "food of the goddess"—chocolate.

Most importantly, attend to the body's desire to be touched and to feel radiantly loved. When you begin to feel that heart chakra spin in the center of your chest—you feel restless and breathless and your heart skips beats when you see your beloved—love is rejoicing. This goddess gate of energy is associated with balance, unconditional love, joy, and acceptance. It emits a glorious bright green color, the color of a new leaf in the sunshine, and exclaims, "I feel!"

To stimulate the heart chakra on yourself or your lover, massage the area over the heart with Love Oil or rose oil, gently circling your fingertips in a counterclockwise motion, eyes closed. Envision the heart, strong and healthy, opening and radiating the earth's richest, most vibrant hue of green.

As your heart chakra opens, the throat chakra responds. The synergy between these two subtle energy centers creates expressive and compassionate communication between you and your lover. You are liberated from the inability to share your thoughts; you no longer feel self-conscious, or are inflicted with a need to exaggerate your truths.

The throat chakra vibrates in a hue of bright blue, the color of the "sky at noon" and is activated by the scent of lavender and chamomile. As you and your lover learn to connect through this energy point, you will begin to be able to "hear" each others' thoughts, almost telepathically. The more in love you become, the less compelled you will be to speak. When the goddess gates of these chakras are open and spinning, a perceptive ecstatician doesn't even need a telephone to communicate long distance.

The Sensuous Picnic

During the season of spring's Enchantment, picnics are, *sans doute,* a catered affair of Aphrodite herself. Become a voluptuary disguised as a cook, and captivate your beloved with sensual seductions of foods and flavors. Choose picnic foods that can be finger-fed; revamp recipes with the trademark flavors and scents dear to the goddess of love, Aphrodite; and illuminate your kitchen with creative playfulness. A goddess knows that the secret ingredient of any dish is love.

These intrepid recipes say, "I dare you."

Jalapeño Applesauce

1 medium jalapeño pepper

4 Golden Delicious or McIntosh apples, peeled, cored, and sliced

1 tablespoon ground cinnamon

¼ teaspoon ground ginger

1 tablespoon rum, optional

½ cup water

After removing the dangerously zesty seeds and ribs, slice the jalapeño lengthwise into 6 to 8 slivers. In a large sauce pan, combine all ingredients.

Cook covered on medium low heat for about 20 minutes or until the apples are mushy.

Remove the jalapeños (if your taste buds are shy) and mash the apples. Serve warm or chilled. Makes one large serving to share.

A Goddess Tip

Jalapeño applesauce tastes great *à la mode*; it will spice up any muffin, provide just the right note for chicken and pork chop dishes, and crown the top of pancakes with ease. Feel free to enjoy however you wish.

Sustain me with raisins,
refresh me with apples; for I am faint with love.
—SONG OF SONGS, 2:5

Ambrosias

With every seductive bite of these cookies, the immortality of love is interwoven with the awareness that there are still spellbinding novelties from beyond this mortal world of which we have yet to dream or taste.

    1 cup butter, room temperature

    1½ cups brown sugar

    ½ cup white sugar

    2 eggs

    1 teaspoon pure vanilla extract

    2 cups unbleached flour

    1 cup oat flour

    ½ teaspoon salt

    ¼ teaspoon baking soda

    ¼ teaspoon baking powder

    1 cup angel-flaked coconut

    1½ cups white chocolate, chopped into chip-sized chunks

    1½ cups walnuts, chopped

    1 cup dried apricots, chopped

Preheat oven to 350° F. In a large mixing bowl, whip up butter and sugars with an electric mixer until fluffy. Add the eggs and vanilla and mix well.

With a fork, blend the salt, baking soda, and baking powder into the measurement of unbleached flour. Tap this flour mixture and the oat flour into the creamed butter and sugar mixture, mixing slowly. Finally, and by hand, stir in the coconut, white chocolate chunks, nut-meats, and apricots.

Line a cookie sheet with baking parchment and scoop the dough with a small (1 to 2 ounce) ice cream scoop. Bake for 10 to 12 minutes, until lightly golden in color with tiny cracks on top of the cookies. Note your baking time for the future. Makes 30 2-ounce sure-to-seduce Ambrosias.

Ambrosias Tip

• Though the oat flour truly is one of the secrets to this buttery wonder, blessing it with a delicate crispy crust, I will admit to making them with all unbleached flour when in the midst of an oat flour shortage. If you do this, remove 1 tablespoon from the total amount of flour used.

> *So are you to my thoughts as food to life,*
> *Or as sweet-season'd showers are to the ground.*
> —SHAKESPEARE, *SONNET LXXV*

Lady Godiva's Riding Secrets

Legends do not agree exactly why and when the lovely Lady Godiva, attired only in her luxurious blonde hair, defied her husband and rode her robust steed down the streets of Coventry. Some say the lofty purpose of her ride was to appease the goddess with her sky-clad beauty; others claim she rode on a dare to abolish a heavy tax. We do know Peeping Tom was struck blind because he gazed upon her, and we are reminded that Lady Godiva set the standard for that enduring bond between girls and their horses.

However, there is an obscure tradition that perhaps explains why today the name "Godiva" is inexorably linked with chocolate in our minds: as she rode languidly along, she held her trademark chocolate creation in hand to avert the attentions of the townsmen. It was really the lady's cake Tom had his sights on, poor guy. In honor of Coventry's favorite horsewoman, I offer you this risqué rendition of her most popular riding accessory.

Lady Godiva's Chocolate Seduction Cake

Crust

1¾ cups (approximately 7 ounces) unsalted pistachio nutmeats, chopped

¼ cup graham cracker crumbs

¼ cup brown sugar

1 teaspoon cinnamon

⅛ teaspoon nutmeg

⅓ cup butter, melted

Filling

27 ounces bittersweet chocolate

$\frac{1}{2}$ cup unsalted butter, room temperature

1 cup white sugar

8 large eggs, room temperature

$\frac{1}{3}$ cup heavy cream

$1\frac{1}{4}$ teaspoon pure vanilla extract

$\frac{1}{3}$ cup Godiva liqueur

For the crust, mix pistachios, graham cracker crumbs, sugar, and spices together. Add butter and mix. Press mixture into the bottom of a 9-inch springform pan. Freeze for at least 30 minutes.

Break chocolate into small pieces and melt in a double boiler until smooth.

In a large bowl, beat butter and sugar together until fluffy. Add eggs, two at a time, beating gently until blended into mixture before adding more eggs. Scrape sides of bowl well and beat mixture on high speed until it increases in volume (approximately 3 minutes).

By hand, whisk melted chocolate (warm but not hot) into the above mixture until creamy. Stir in cream, vanilla, and Godiva liqueur. Pour mixture into crust and chill for at least 6 hours before serving. Makes enough cake to seduce at least 10 admirers.

God, grant us our desires and grant them swiftly.
—Catherine the Great

The Loveliest of Letters

 goddess in love is a mistress of the word . . . written in love letters. To enhance the seductive effects of your communications, there is a fine art to becoming a skilled courtesan of this timeless love art.

- *Appeal to your lover's senses.* Choose paper or media that is an enticing color; perfume your paper; use textured paper that delights the sense of touch; write with a colored pen.

- *Keep your love letters brief and intimate.* Use the word *you* as often as possible, especially in sentences graced by the word *I*. Describe not only your feelings, but how he looks, physically, in your eyes. Empower him with words like *handsome, virile, strong,* and *manly*.

- *Deliver your letters in clever ways.* Have a friend hand-deliver it; attach it to an apple pie; tape it on the back window of his car so he discovers it in the rearview mirror; send it via Climax or Loveland, Colorado, for a postmark of promise.

- *Light a red candle when you send the letter;* allow it to burn for one hour. Then, when you believe he has received it, relight the same candle and visualize him reading it. Always wait three days before writing another love letter. This allows activation time for the spell of each individual letter to be diffused.

- *Never send a love letter via e-mail.* The letter will lack the depth of your intention, the energy of your vibrations, and the beauty of your hand. E-mail notes tend to be littered with misspellings and impulsive, un-thought-out words. A computer is like a third person in your relationship, and we all know "two is company—three's an orgy." Resist the convenient temptation of succumbing to technological lust.

- *Always S.W.A.K., if not more.* The goddess in love will use her unabashed imagination with this final stroke—and blessing—of her love letter.

Words of Gold

Words are not to be wasted; and I have wasted
so many on so many men.
—CLEOPATRA

In comparison to her mortal sisters who have not quite acquired divine status in affairs of the heart, a goddess in love speaks consciously and truthfully, knowing well the power of her words. Sometimes in whimsical moments of carefree thought, a fantasy takes verbal form or you make a promise you have no conscious intention of keeping. The season of Enchantment, with its influence of a the coquettish waxing moon and increasing passion, offers endless situations where such temptations arise. In such cases, beware the repercussions of carelessness. Though your purpose was never to hurt your lover, the goddess Nemesis listens in on these conversations. And no one, god or goddess, can escape her judgment.

When you make promises you cannot keep, Nemesis reappears in times of decision and challenge, holding the fruits of your words—and actions—of which you must taste; bitter is the fruit of false words. Love is delicate and hearts are fragile. Do not betroth your undying eternal love if in reality you are simply floating on a wave of momentary ecstasy and feel compelled to profess your caprice. Because when the time arrives to play your hand in love, your unintentional bluff will hurt, as would a bluff a lover called on you.

A goddess in love listens attentively to words, and learns not to confuse confetti with gold. Though it is essential for you to open yourself to love's Enchantment and remove any leftover heart-armor, you must be wise. In their quest to comprehend love's mystery and magnificence, your mortal paramours may make mistakes and speak vaporous words, too. Give them to Nemesis for her dose of divine justice; never deplete your energy with plotting revenge.

Why Is She Smiling?

Beware of too many questions during this season of love. A goddess never inquires about past lovers (it does not interest her) and rarely answers when asked about hers. There are certain questions a goddess learns to answer with only a smile, leaving the "burden of truth" on her inquisitor:

How old are you? (A gentlemen should never ask);

What are you doing tonight? (A goddess needs more than a day to prepare—besides, what business is it of his unless he intends to invite you to do something with him; in that case he must learn to word the question properly);

Do you want to make love?

A Goddess' Partner Primer

There are two basic types of men: the *Goddess-kissed* and the *Goddess-dissed.* A goddess-kissed man has felt the embrace of the divine feminine at some point in his life. Consequently, he is secure with himself and comfortable with the natural presence of a woman. He respects her beliefs and accepts her for who she is. He strives to understand her, refrains from being cynical in love, is playful and patient, does not fear her feminine power, and loves the vibration of women in general. There is a very good chance he had or has a healthy relationship with his mother, the first goddess in his life. He is eager and intrigued and easy to educate. He sincerely wants to know about the mysteries of a woman's heart.

The goddess-dissed stands in awe of a woman, not knowing exactly how to handle her. He may have had negative experiences with women or had a mother who was an unfulfilling role model, absent or demeaning. He may be filled with an imprinted mistrust of feminine energy. He *says* he wants to know about the mysteries of a woman's heart, but is either not ready, subconsciously fearful, or still too involved in his own needs to draw from a woman's power.

With all the right touches, both types of lovers, of course, make exceptional consorts. A goddess who is inspired to keep a golden glove on the heart-and-soul beat of her lover can redeem the love of any blessed relationship. However, a goddess-dissed gentleman needs time and space to gather his courage to approach a frisky goddess like you. Never pursue this man (rarely, if ever, pursue *any* man!); he will retreat like a jackrabbit. If he is the soulmate that you attracted and the universe approved of, be assured he will advance on his turf in his time—your intuition will tell you if you have the patience to dally; you can always date others while waiting. When you are playing in love together, you must introduce him to the powers of the moon patiently and gently, taking care not to overwhelm him with your wildness.

Both goddess-kissed and goddess-dissed paramours flourish when loved by a goddess who speaks the truth, gently and directly. For in your respectful honesty, you share peace with your partner. And a lover at peace with himself will be at peace with you. Always leave lines open for honest peace talks.

Any time that is not spent on love is wasted.
—TORQUATO TASSO

Words and Images of Enchantment

A Fine Romance by Judith Sills
Camille by Alexander Dumas
"Song of Songs," the Bible
Still Life with Woodpecker by Tom Robbins
Through the Looking-Glass by Lewis Carroll
Victoria magazine

Love Tips

♥ The secret of loving begins with a smile. When you smile, your heart experiences a momentary burst of joy and consequently the force of love is literally pumped through your cells. In that delicious twinkling of time you lay down your "sword and shield" and you radiate light. And remember, a smile graces your face with more beauty and luminosity than the best work of the most renowned cosmetic surgeon. So smile!

♥ "Music is the deep shudder of the soul in enchantment." Thus spoke wiseman Einstein. Love has always lain its heart on a "pillow of music," from the days of the troubadours who cooed their "woman songs" (so potent, they were forbidden to be sung in medieval church) to the days of Smokey Robinson. Let your life be filled with music: Listen to *live* music with your lover at least once during the moon's cycle; acquire appreciation for his favorite music; introduce him to your favorite "woman songs."

Record your "Personal Soundtrack of Enchantment", a best-of anthology of songs that evoke feelings of love's bliss and innocence in you—songs you swooned to in high school or that echo times of peaceful, happy yesterdays. Listen to your tape when you jog or play it when you bathe. Whether your favorite tunes are sung by Frank Sinatra, The Partridge Family, or The Grateful Dead, listening to your soundtrack will keep you on track of the "best of" love's beat.

Build a bonfire on a warm night under the new crescent moon in May. Be the May Queen. Dance with you lover around the fire and then invite him to play the goddess' version of "Jack Be Nimble, Jack Be Quick" by taking turns jumping over the fire (taking care not to ignite the goods). This ancient *a-Maying* game of fire leaping is said to bring good luck in relationships. With each jump, make a wish that love can fulfill.

Pen a collection entitled "The Sensual Sutra" for your beloved. A *sutra* (which means "thread" in Sanskrit) is like a cosmic axiom of goddess wisdom or a self-evident truth— ultimately a universal truth—that you weave through the fabric of your beliefs. Purchase a beautiful notebook that feels good to hold in your hand and a special pen reserved for your writing. In time you will give him this book as a gift; but it also serves to highlight your truths in love and lend awareness to the gifts of enchantment. My favorite is *"The secret to loving is loving."* Other sensual sutras that come to mind are, *"To have passion in love, you must have passion in life,"* and *"Happiness is our only function."*

♍ Blindfold your lover with a yellow silk scarf and give him a foot massage with Love Oil (recipe on page 55), followed by a sensuous scalp massage. No spoken spell is necessary for this enchantment.

♍ There are three aspects of a man which you *must* know before you make love to him: (1) his mother's name; (2) his favorite food; and (3) his birthday. The first two are self-explanatory. However, to know *him,* it is invaluable for a goddess to explore the astrological aspects of her paramour. Though the placement of his sun is important—is he a Fire Man, Water Man, Earth Man, or Air Man?—so is the position of his moon and Venus, the planet that rules his ways in love. Have his (and your) complete chart cast. Then take an astrology class or consult an astrologer who specializes in synastry and composite charts (I consult with Robert Blanchard, 530-546-5999) to examine the aspects of the "star" you create together. Are you conjunct? Trine?

Twin flames? Remember, Free Will and Fate are unlikely lovers, yet they exist in a divine union, inseparable. Who you attract is a mirror of yourself, so any sign—Water Man or Magic Man—can work.

Memorize the words to "Stairway to Heaven" by Led Zeppelin; listen to this anthem of enchantment, mystery, and power and use its message in weaving your love spells. *Be* the "lady who shines white light."

The Enchantment of love *inspires* you.

> *I wish for you all good things life has to offer:*
> *Health, happiness, dreams fulfilled,*
> *and a lifetime of rich adventure.*
> —THOMAS E. TRUMBLE

CHAPTER 4

The Passion

Ascending in Summer's Ecstasy

Love Heats Up

She's got everything delightful
She's got everything I need
A breeze in the pines in the summer night moonlight
Crazy in the sunlight, yes, indeed. . . .
—ROBERT HUNTER, "SUGAR MAGNOLIA"

The universal, timeless truth is that passion fortified with all the magic of divine enchantment and championed by the insights of the soul is more likely to endure than passion born of mortal impulse. If you honor the gifts of this season, you are promised a passion that will return—eternally igniting itself within you—with each full moon, with every summer breeze, and each time you light a candle and feel your senses stir. Remember, a goddess does not lose her balance and bearings when love comes to town. Rather, she ascends in love with a light and blissful spirit, knowing her heart must be buoyant and inspired so that her passions can soar! This is what separates the girls from the goddesses.

The Passion of summer is the easiest season of love for most to glide into and the most difficult to sustain. In fact, many women skip the Vision altogether, shortchange themselves of the Enchantment, and leap, blindly, into the Passion. Overwhelmed with what Emerson described as "divine rage and enthusiasm," and no wiser than a radar-impaired luna moth during this sexual frenzy, our sightless sisters are impelled toward the fiery light of the flame. Throbbing, succulent, and wildly tipsy on the nectars of the human sex hormone *alpha androsterole,* they ignite feverishly . . . and too soon fizzle.

We watch them trip and sizzle before the coolness of autumn's flowing serenity comes to soothe their souls; the key to the Celebration has been lost somewhere in the cold morning ashes. They are not in the playing fields of the goddess. They are being mortally careless, forfeiting their fragile bond with their goddess-muse and their own integrity, choosing rather to reel in fast-forward into the inferno of obsession.

To these ungraceful girls who are "lost in lust," I plead, "Quickly, dive into a lake of cold, clear water, lie down and allow the massive, marvelous arms of the sunshine to embrace and warm your body . . . and breathe. *Breathe.* Then, imagine your dream-beloved pouring wild mountain honey slowly over your smooth, golden breasts until its viscous river glistens past your ribs and forms a golden pool in the hollow of your navel. Imagine your lover tasting the honey with trembling lips, his shadow dancing over you as he kisses your stomach, kisses your neck."

The defining moment of love's Passion will transform you. In a flash of divine rapture, a truth becomes absolute and there is no denying it: you desire true love. With his soulful kiss, the music of your soul swirls in sunburst passion and a message of adoration and devotion is etched into your cells by roaring whispers. By this comforting communion of touch you blossom into yourself, radiant and streaming, enlivened by compassion's torch. A newborn beauty swells within you and all of passion's mysteries are yours to hail. You are soaring to rare heights of ecstasy and fulfillment, supported by the ancient wiles and wisdom of all the goddesses.

The first sigh of love is the last of wisdom.
—BOVÉE

The Goddess' Dance of Passion

A goddess in love ascends through her passion, lifted by the divine feminine power that surrounds her. This is the bold sexuality of Ishtar and the smoldering power of Pele of the Islands, tempered by the buoyant resilience of Selene, the Greek goddess of the moon, sister of the sun. Laughing and alive in love, Selene pulls the full moon across the south skies while its banner trails in the delicious light of the night, exclaiming "Surrender goddess!" The Graces attend to the lovers, singing of joy, charm, and beauty, while the great Tantric goddess Shakti ("cosmic energy") looks on approvingly, infusing all lovemaking with her infinite and mysterious power.

The goddess Ishtar shows herself in the platinum light of night as a woman who knows the power of her sexuality, and receives her consorts when she is prepared and pleased. Historically related to Mary Magdelene through her persona of Mari-Ishtar, she is also the great harlot, mistress of ecstasy, who anointed her god with holy oil before his death and symbolic descent to the shadows followed by his resurrection three days later. She too understands the multidimensional prism of love's light as it swirls restlessly amid mortal passion, casting both color and shadow.

We are also reminded of the consequences of dancing lustily in this season of sexual power and transformation. The wild and unapproachable fire goddess Pele, whose hair is woven with molten lava of a trembling volcano, represents the anger that may confront you in any stage of love; she warns you not to push your true feelings down inside until they erupt uncontrollably. She commands her passions.

In another light, you are cautioned of the fruits of lust. Caught within love's web and inflamed by the light of the moon and the heat of the season, Eros, god of love seduces the beautiful Psyche—even Aphrodite was jealous of the princess' loveliness—and a daughter Voluptua ("pleasure") is born to them. In the summer of love, no one is beyond the call of passion.

> *Give me my Romeo, and when he shall die*
> *Take him and cut him out in little stars,*
> *and he will make the face of heaven so fine,*
> *And all the world will be in love with night. . . .*
> —SHAKESPEARE, *ROMEO AND JULIET*

The Sizzle of the Summer Solstice

Midsummer Night, the shortest night of the year, is always illumined with great bonfires, the "flames of courage," usually lit near bodies of water to symbolize the balance needed in this season: heat and coolness, fire and water, the polarities of love's wheel. As with May Day celebrations, fire-leaping games continue, and lovers gather to share their positive strengths and work magic for increased energy and clarity of thoughts.

This is also the time of the ancient ritual of handfasting (also called "hand-fastening" or trysting, a derivative of "trusting"), a spiritual ceremony joining two people in sacred union. Handfasting tradition transcends the dictates of contractual marriage in the sense that it recognizes an *eternal* bonding of souls within the birth-death-rebirth cycle of the natural world, far beyond "from death do us part." Two lovers pledge their promise of trust while firmly holding each other's hands wrapped tightly in a blessed, often specially embroidered, cloth (remember *Braveheart*?).

Celebrations of love and intrigue abound; midnight picnics in the full moon are frequented by the midsummer night's fairies who seek unsuspecting lovers to tease and bewilder. Aware and ready for adventure, the goddess in love cultivates her voluptuous charms.

Subtle Seduction of the Senses

A goddess is an artisan in creating an atmosphere of intrigue and seduction wherever she moves. When entertaining a lover, evoking a desirable mood is essential to procure attentions and heighten passions. In the fiery season of summer, passion's shades of ecstasy—red, deep red, bright red, garnet, pink, and silver (the banner of Selene)—beg to be unfurled and displayed. Red is the color of fire and blood; both are alive and fascinating, both signal danger. Red first attracts the eye, and then the body is drawn to it.

Contemplate a few bewitching tips from one of history's greatest of courtesans—Cleopatra was renowned for her seductive wit. It is said she sunbathed with rubies over her eyes, and enjoyed dining with Marc Anthony amid the pageantry of lovely servants who wore strawberries on their nipples while serving aphrodisiac delicacies. This enchantress was a magician at capturing all of her lover's senses. He was satiated with tastes of rich foods, his eyes feasted upon his queen's exotic beauty, and his mind was infused with her erotic, mood-enhancing perfumes.

The ancient Egyptians were goddesses of aromatherapy, and are believed be the first to distill the substances of plants and flowers into essential oils. Scents of sandalwood, cinnamon, patchouli, rose, ylang-ylang, vanilla, and musk were extremely valuable and have always been used liberally to entice the mind and trigger bodily responses. A goddess in love keeps these keys to passion's gate near at hand in the form of incense, massage oils, bath oils, and perfumes . . . and uses them skillfully during full moons and during the summer season of love.

Lady in Red

To incite desire in a paramour, decorate your life with every possible shade of "love red" imaginable. Plant a botanical masterpiece of vibrant flowers in your garden, fill crystal vases with roses, and blanket your bed and bath with fragrant petals; stock your wine rack with favorite vintages of blood-red wines; and display lavish bowls of strawberries, apples, and vine-ripened tomatoes—the original love apples. If you wear red well, treat yourself to a bright, flowing dress or comfortably sexy lingerie. Indulge in the deepest, most luscious shade of ruby lipstick your kissable lips can sport.

Sensual Super Glue Spell

If you want to try a powerful, extra-credit, simple love spell, this is a contemporary, sure-fire recipe for enchanting a lover. I call it the "Sensual Super Glue Spell."

- Before you begin the spell, have a mutual, respected friend tell your lover that you like *him* (not love, *like*); keep this step nice and simple; it activates the magic.

- On the next full moon, go into a small, candlelit room for one hour together with your lover and a bottle of red wine or a crystal pitcher of ice water and a power token to hold, such as a stick, a wand, or a large crystal. While holding the token, take turns exchanging the most intimate information you can bear to share. Maybe tell him you really do kiss frogs or mention your fear of kissing with your eyes open. Talk about the most embarrassing moment of your life, or what you would grab in case of a fire—these types of things. Each person speaks for three minutes and then passes the token to the other. Continue for an hour. The person listening can never interrupt the person talking.

- When the hour has passed, sit facing each other and stare into each other's eyes for two minutes without talking. No talking!

- Give the token to your lover as a cosmic keepsake; it has been enriched with the power of your secrets. Now go for a walk in the moonlight. Have faith—the spell is cast.

Jewel in the Lotus

God and sex are the only two things
that really interest me.
—H. G. WELLS

In the height of summer's passion, the navel/sacral chakra spins determinedly, emitting a glowing, burning orange, the color of a sunset on a hot humid day. When this energy center (directly below your navel) is balanced, it acts to empower sexual vitality and the ability to enjoy the tactile and sensual pleasures of your body. *Wanting* and *touching*, the favorite preoccupations under a smiling, full moon, now manifest in a universal translation of the divine act—*Om mani padme om*—Jewel in the Lotus—*lingam* in the *yoni*—Diamond Scepter in the Goddess Gate—you get the idea.

The primary Tantric focus of worship (yes, goddesses, *worship*) and source of divine energy is the *yoni*, a woman's vulva. As explained in the *Women's Encyclopedia of Myths and Secrets* by Barbara G. Walker, "The basic principle of Tantrism was that women possess more spiritual energy than men, and a man could achieve realization of the divinity only through sexual and emotional union with a woman." This sacred energy, or *kundalini*, is the essence of the goddess Shakti, coiled like a serpent (now we know why they told us Eve was tempted by a snake) at the base of the spine. When aroused by chakra meditation and stimulation or Tantric discipline, she ascends through the spinal column, stimulates the woman's sacred spot as she passes, and manifests her power in the sacral chakra as divine orgasm.

Of course, the male energy of Shiva, symbolized by his great sacred phallus—Thor's thunderbolt, the spark of life, the "ambassador"—becomes emblazoned by this cosmic "force of intercourse" and achieves its own explosive union with the divine. In lore, wherever Shiva's *lingam* went (attached to him, of course), miracles abounded. The miracle of sex is that it can fortify and deepen love. A wise goddess of passion embraces this mystery, thus empowering her lover's great miracle worker—and his ego—with her attentions and talents as often as she desires. The power is hers to share.

The miracle of passionate love, blessed by the goddess, is that you are willing to trust completely another person and surrender your whole self to him, yet remain whole. The Shakti energy of this union travels in the circle of balance through the body's chakras and into the spirits of both lovers, fortifying their strengths and whisking all deficiencies into the genesis of a pure soul in ecstasy. In this fire of natural passion between a man and woman, powerful magic is interwoven into every glance, every movement, every act of love. You honor and exalt the differences in each other while recognizing the sacred and valued energy of being both animal and divine. The god and goddess are one, and you are love.

The greatest lover in the world cannot give a woman
an orgasm unless she allows herself to have it.
But men dream on.
—Dr. Ruth Westheimer

Ishtar's Sensual Magic

Take a lesson in pleasure from the divine courtesan Ishtar and her sacred temple girls, the Ishtaritu and *qadishtu* (the holy ones). These mistresses of sensual magic, who reserved their sexual powers to appease their goddess, would perform elaborate rituals on chosen (and lucky) male worshipers in her temples, schooling them on the sexual mysteries. Also known as *horae* (ladies of the hour), named for Aphrodite's celestial nymphs, these skilled priestesses could "heal" with their touch.

In honor of Ishtar, bestow your powers upon your lover. Draw a perfectly temperate footbath filled with Epsom salts and drops of a favorite essential oil or oil blend (try a combination of rose and cardamom, Cleopatra's signature scent). Bathe your lover's feet, slowly and attentively. Sing a soulful ballad while you massage the tender soles of his feet and between his toes. When you are finished, dry his feet with your hair, a la an Ishtaritu. With every stroke of your hair and every kiss to your beloved's ecstatic feet, you are fulfilling a sacred vow to the goddess and to the happiness of the one you love.

Fertility and Other Sexual Rights

*O*ne can hardly regard the passion of love without thinking of sex; and sex should not be considered without heeding its consequences. The momentary ecstasy of divine (or mortal) union can have profound consequences, most notably the creation of life. A goddess is fully aware of this power and does not ponder it lightly. From season to season, lover to lover, situation to situation, she revamps and revitalizes her methods of birth control and *always* practices "safe sex"—using condoms *unfailingly*—when sampling the sexual universe.

All goddess should learn about their natural cycles and tune into their times and phases of fertility. Many women who menstruate on the new moon will ovulate on the full moon. Up to five days before you ovulate and for a day or two afterward, you can conceive. Regardless of the method you use, you should *own* this knowledge; it is your body.

If you are in a secure and supportive relationship, I wholeheartedly encourage the use of natural birth control methods such as the sympto-thermal method, which is based on observing changes in cervical mucous and basal temperatures throughout your monthly cycle. This method can always be fortified by using a condom (which must always be used with "newer" lovers anyway), a cervical cap, spermicide, and/or the ol' midnight trampoline—the diaphragm. When a goddess becomes a mistress of this method, it is more effective than the Pill. Ironically, Catholic nuns and church laywomen often teach this natural method, so why not call your local church?

Though it is ultimately a woman's choice to make, I do not hold chemical, hormonal methods of birth control, such as the Pill, Norplant, or Depo-Provera in high esteem. I honestly believe such chemicals often suspend a woman's ability to feel her body's natural tempo; thus in subtle ways they separate her from her innate goddess power. As an ovulatory guinea pig in a research study on a new triphasal pill long ago, I noticed, in addition to all the disturbing physical side-effects, that my dreams changed. I stopped taking the drugs immediately. Years later, when I was pregnant, I had those same hormonally tweaked dreams; giving birth to my daughter—and rebirth to my own dreams—was a double blessing. So goddesses, be aware and please don't let carelessness interfere with your dreams.

Leap Where Angels Fear to Tread

The sexual urge is stronger than the fear of death.
—WILHELM REICH

To be able to flow wholeheartedly with love's seasons and the influences of the capricious, ever-changing yet constant moon, you have to feed your masculine animal self, your "soul-force," your *animus*. As Clarissa Pinkola Estes asserts in her popular book *Women Who Run with the Wolves*, "*Animus* can best be understood as a force that assists women in acting in their own behalves. . . . *Animus* helps a woman put forth her specific and feminine inner thoughts and feelings in concrete ways—emotionally, sexually, financially, creatively, and otherwise."

A goddess twirling through the season of passionate love knows the importance of letting her wild woman drink from a clean river to soothe, nourish, and cleanse her body soul and mind. She nurtures her own creative life before she attends to the sanctification of her lover. (As my friend says, "Stay in your own lane and move forward.") She never loses touch with her truth that all love stems from self-love. She consciously runs her own energy and is careful not to take on the burdens of her lover, thus depriving him of the gift of working out his own salvation with care. She keeps her "river"—her source of divine, creative inspiration—unblocked and flowing, never letting it become polluted with pressures from her culture or her lover. She stays free to love in the most sacred sense.

To ascend to goddess status in love, you must be fully prepared to acknowledge that you alone create and attract all the experiences in your life, including and most importantly, the relationship with your lover (with a few twists thrown in by the Fates). Yes, of course, when you are basking in the divine lovelight with your beloved, you certainly coauthor your love story together. But when times of conflict arise (and with Pele dancing in the moonlight of love's Passion, they will), a goddess goes straight to her proverbial magic mirror and asks, "Mirror, mirror, of life's flow, tell me what I need to know." She *never* blames a lover for circumstances that she has either created or allowed to manifest in her life.

Unless a situation involves a despicable breach of honor and respect of a woman by a worm of a man, such as rape, abuse, or kidnapping (in this case, turn him over to "Maman Brigette" with the spellwork outlined on pages 199 and 200 in Luisah Teish's book *Jambalaya*), a woman blessed with goddess power cannot be taken advantage of unless she allows it. Regardless of *all other circumstances*, the goddess-graced woman must learn to acknowledge her role in every move she makes with her consort, and must take full responsibility for the "serious scenes she creates." If you find yourself in the habit of doing something or acting in a way that is uncomfortable or frustrating (i.e., exposing yourself to unrequited love), you must make a full, conscious, positive decision grounded in your goddess within and *make a change*. It is this simple. Just say "Know."

Mystic Transformation Meditation

*E*very day for six minutes, create a sense of self that is glowing, perfected, cleansed, redeemed, shining with bliss—a center of grace; a place in your soul where all cravings are satiated, all problems resolved (the Latin root of *resolve* is *solvere*, which means "release"). Close your eyes, breathe, calm the mind chatter, enter into yourself—the temple of the soul—and whisper all or part of this powerful incantation as the powers of the Earth and skies and universe listen:

Come holy spirit-goddess
beloved of my soul,
I beseech you to
enlighten me, guide me, fill me with love,
whisper your will into my heart,
fill my soul with vision.

We must be married directly and go to Italy.
—ROBERT BROWNING

Traveling with your lover can be an incredible aphrodisiac. It also offers a fast lane to becoming acquainted—for the better, I hope. When you travel with a paramour you discover his assets and hang-ups quicker than you can say, "How do I love thee? Let me count the ways . . ." in Swahili. To a goddess, an exquisite road-buddy is golden.

Begin your travels together by daydreaming about the places you would like to explore. Let your mind fly freely about the world; time, finances, and language barriers are not a concern. Then, without consulting each other, write down your "seven wonders of the world" list and ask him to write down seven hot spots that interest him. Compare notes.

Did you both envision bungee jumping in the rainforests of Australia, or perhaps sharing a plate of fresh calamari on the Adriatic coast of Croatia? Kissing in Paris? Skiing in Aspen? Cheering at a Notre Dame football game in South Bend, Indiana? No? Take heart; if you can't agree on a getaway destination, the goddess has one word of advice: *Italia.*

Making Love for Dinner

The sight of her face . . . together with the maddening fragrance
of food, evoked an emotion of a wild tenderness
and hunger in him which was unutterable.
—THOMAS WOLFE, *APRIL, LATE APRIL*

The onset of a full moon evening ushers in a charismatic transformation of perspective: the demands of the day melt behind the horizon; the winds change or become silent; your imagination is enhanced, often intoxicated by the sensations of the night. You have entered the silvery realm of Selene, goddess of the full moon, enchantress of the palate.

The aphrodisiac foods of night nourish and excite in their own fashion; the sense of taste seems to take on a life of its own when accompanied by candlelight, starlight, and moonlight. The food rituals of lovers become deliciously taboo, seasoned with teasing and mystery. You feed each other with *all* your fingers, drink champagne straight from the bottle, and forfeit your membership in the "Clean Plate Club" for an impromptu invitation to make love on the table. But a goddess and her consort cannot live on ambrosia and pomegranate seeds alone. In this light, I offer you an entrée of unfettered panache, which of course can be prepared in the reason of daylight and warmed for the occasion. While dining on Aphrodite's seductive marquis dishes of seafood with vanilla sauce, savor the sumptuous sexuality of Selene's light and enjoy your full moon feast with your lover.

Les Crêpes Parfait

1 cup flour

3 eggs

1½ cups milk

1 tablespoon sugar

¼ teaspoon ground nutmeg

⅛ teaspoon salt

2 tablespoons butter, melted

2 teaspoons dark rum (optional)

Whisk eggs, milk, sugar, nutmeg, and salt together. Slowly add flour and stir until smooth. Add melted butter, and rum if desired, and whisk together until frothy. Let batter stand for one to two hours before using.

Heat a small skillet or seasoned crêpe pan over medium-high heat. Brush lightly with butter before preparing each crêpe. Pour approximately ¼ cup of the batter into the pan and immediately swirl it around to coat the bottom of the pan. When the crêpe begins to "puff," flip it over and cook a few seconds more. Remove from pan. Stack the crêpes and keep covered until ready to roll. Makes 6 crêpes.

Le Sauté

1 pound bay scallops

2 to 3 mushrooms, sliced

Le Sauté (continued)

1 tablespoon butter (optional)

Juice of $\frac{1}{2}$ lime

1 tablespoon olive oil

1 green bell pepper, diced

1 red bell pepper, diced

1 yellow bell pepper, diced

$\frac{1}{2}$ medium red onion, finely chopped

1 clove garlic, minced

1 tablespoon brown sugar

Vanilla Sauce

$\frac{1}{2}$ cup vegetable broth, clam juice, or seafood stock

2 tablespoons white wine or apple cider

1 tablespoon flour

$\frac{3}{4}$ teaspoon pure vanilla extract

1 tablespoon fresh basil, minced

$\frac{1}{2}$ teaspoon salt

$\frac{1}{4}$ teaspoon paprika

A few dashes of Tabasco

$\frac{2}{3}$ cup cream or evaporated milk

$\frac{1}{2}$ cup cheese of your choice, grated (I like Swiss)

Paprika for garnish

In the largest skillet in the house, sauté scallops and mushrooms in lime juice (and butter, if desired) for 2 minutes. Remove and set aside. In the same pan, heat olive oil over medium-high heat. Stir in peppers, onion, garlic, and sugar, and sauté for 3 to 4 minutes.

Then add stock and white wine (or apple juice) and bring to a reduction boil. When this begins, sprinkle in flour while stirring constantly. Add vanilla, basil, salt, paprika, and Tabasco, and sauté for another minute. Stir in cream. Bring the sauce to a rolling boil and cook for a few more minutes.

Return the scallop and mushroom sauté to the sauce and cook for 2 more minutes; then turn heat to very low. Using a slotted spoon, measure enough scallop mixture to fill a crêpe (about ⅓ cup per crêpe), allowing the sauce to drain back into the pan. Roll the crêpes and place side by side, seam hidden, in an ovenproof casserole or serving dish.

Spoon the remaining warm vanilla sauce over the crêpes, sprinkle with cheese and paprika, and bake at 400° F for 7 minutes. (I've also had luck using a microwave on HIGH for 1 to 2 minutes.) Garnish with fresh parsley sprigs and serve with an unpretentious but powerful vegetable, such as steamed asparagus. Serves 2.

Like sex, cooking is a living artform which inspires you to indulge in instant gratification with those you love, while capturing their attention, appetites, and yes, even their hearts.
—MICHAEL J. BEISER

Key Lime Luna Pie

To secure the potency of this luscious, creamy pie, prepare it while naked—"sky-clad" as we spell-mixing sibyls say. To transfix the charm on your beloved, spoon-feed it to him, reclining, in the light of a full moon.

> 1 prepared graham cracker, chocolate Oreo cookie, or vanilla wafer pie crust
>
> 1 8-ounce package cream cheese, room temperature
>
> 1 12-ounce can sweetened condensed milk
>
> ½ cup real key lime juice
>
> 1 cup whipped cream or prepared whipped cream topping

Either prepare a pie crust according to a favorite recipe or purchase one that is already prepared (more time for kissing). My favorite crust for this pie is the chocolate Oreo cookie crust.

If using "real" whipped cream, whip cream until stiff. In another large bowl, combine cream cheese and milk and whip together until smooth. Beat in key lime juice. Gently fold in whipped cream. Pour ingredients into pie shell and chill for at least one hour (you can put it in the freezer for a quick chill if desired). Always taste your first bite of this pie with your eyes closed. It's sensational!

An aphrodisiac is anything you think it is.
—Dr. Ruth Westheimer

Spiritual Sunscreen

A woman's heart is a deep ocean of secrets.
—ROSE DAWSON CALVERT, *TITANIC*

As you gracefully accept love's gifts and your heart's achievements, secrets—those intuitive whisperings (or shoutings!) from the center of your soul—emerge to guide you to the next level of communion with your beloved. Secrets are the soul's sunscreen, serving to protect you and those you love from the rays of others' judgments and dictates.

Unfortunately, it is not uncommon to have family, friends, or acquaintances who want more than a sideline seat to observe your relationship. Many of these people secretly desire to participate in your courtship by giving unwanted advice, casting pro-or-con spells of their own on your union (or your lover), or inadvertently confusing you with their vibrations of envy or jealousy. As a goddess, transcend. Simply learn to smile knowingly, hold your head up and your eyes ahead, and unapologetically apply "Joe's Secret Code."

Don't waste your secrets on people who:

(1) are not *able* to understand;

(2) do not *want* to understand;

(3) don't *deserve* to know.

As Sonia Choquette reminds us in her book *Your Heart's Desire*, "Remember there's power in secrecy. Keep your dreams protected by silence." Apply spiritual sunscreen when necessary and you will never get burned.

The Full Moon's Cosmic Messages

January	*Wolf Moon*—a time to honor the strength of the spirit.	
February	*Snow Moon*—a time of quiet vision and purity of intention.	
March	*Sap or Worm Moon*—a time to honor the life-force of the earth.	
April	*Pink Moon*—a time of health and vitality.	
May	*Flower Moon*—in celebration of beauty and inspiration.	
June	*Strawberry Moon*—here, the sweetness of life sustains us.	
July	*Thunder Moon*—in honor of nourishing rains and the recharging power of storms.	
August	*Red Moon*—a sensual time of passion.	
September	*Harvest Moon*—time to reap the thoughts, actions, words, and plans we have sown.	
October	*Hunter's Moon*—a time to honor the need of physical nourishment.	
November	*Beaver Moon*—a time to receive the gifts of our wild nature.	
December	*Cold Moon*—rekindle the flame in our hearts and souls.	

Love Lessons of Lammas

The celebration of Lammas in the goddess' love calendar marks the transformation of summer's frolic to a vulnerable period of decision and reckoning. Traditionally honored on August 1, this holiday, which means the "Feast of Bread," reflects the numbered days of summer when change is imminent. Grapes are being made into wine, the newly harvested wheat is being baked into bread; bread is being broken and shared in ritual communion.

In affairs of the heart, this is a time when the flow of feelings subtly begins to change its course. As the momentum of summer's passion switches gear and the moon begins to wane, the zealous energy of lovers naturally changes too. In this season of "the Switch," your heart urges you to look toward a love that is pure, focused, and inspired. You desire a sacred communion of two bodies, two lives, two spirits.

The decisions you make during this season of love are often the most significant and consequential. Your thoughts, actions, words, and desires during this time adjust the tempo for the future of your relationship. Because you are still infused with the ecstasy and immortality of passion, reason is challenged; because the natural essence of your soul is calling you to create a future which nourishes and sustains—with or without your current lover in your arms—passion is checked. The fires of love, though still burning, will inevitably change as the season changes; some will be transformed into enduring, warming embers from which future flames can grow; others will cool. The reassuring power of the goddess and promise of love's eventual rebirth must be evoked now to inspire you to move gracefully through this transition.

A kiss is just a kiss—not a contract.
—STELLA RESNICK, *THE PLEASURE ZONE*

There's Always Hope

Iris, the goddess of the rainbow, appears on Earth as advisor and guide to convey divine messages and decrees to all lovers who seek her. Her greatest message has always been hope; she is always there—*somewhere* in the universe—holding all the mysteries of love to help you feel peace in your heart. This radiant maiden with beautiful prismatic wings always appears when you need her most, heralding the passing storm with a rainbow of promise and hope trailing across the sky in her wake.

Hail Goddess, Full of Grace

Before you are free to saunter into love's next season of Celebration, you must assess whether your love for your paramour—and his for you—is beyond the illusion of passion's fires and capable of supporting the foundation of commitment: a shared life, a life together as best friends in love. If it is not, this could be the time for a goddess in love to securely embrace herself, call on the power of the Graces, and honor Goddess Rule of Love #4: *Learn to release gracefully and gratefully with divine timing.* Here, the three Graces—the triple embodiment of dignity and beauty—will soothe and counsel you. Thalia, the goddess of good cheer, will lighten your spirit; Aglaia, goddess of splendor, will reassure you of the creative beauty of the universe; and the goddess of mirth, Euphrosyne, will attend to your heart and fill it with joys of the past, present, and future.

The season of passion can continue beyond its days if you fail to accept your lover's reluctance to give a vow of love. If this happens, you must hold your head up, take a deep breath, and recognize your playmate as the quintessential summer love. He may be someone whose sensuous company is exciting, smoldering, pleasurable, perhaps lighthearted and fun, but not the person the Fates have set their sights on as your soulmate. In all ultimate fairness, this is a soul—person, friend, lover, boy-toy, or fantasy man—you must "give back to the angels." A goddess of grace would never expect a lover to forgo his beliefs to fulfill her own. And, "I love you *if...*" is not love. Elizabeth-Kübler Ross has said if you find yourself saying "I love you *if...*, bite your lip until it bleeds."

Knowing when to gracefully say "Thank you and good-bye" is perhaps the most difficult but most respectful and loving act you can learn. Understanding this and cultivating the strength and wisdom to "let go and let goddess" is what separates mortal women and goddesses-in-training from true goddesses of love. A goddess does not make promises under the influence of hormones and lust that she cannot or will not keep. Therefore, if honesty and the thoughtful constraint of not "acting out" your romantic notions and fantasies by making flighty promises were an honorable basis for your summer-love fling,

dissolving physical and emotional bonds can be a time of completion, gratitude, and unconditional love.

You do not have to stop loving someone when you give him back to the
angels. You are simply releasing his soul to its highest good and allowing him
the opportunity to seek his own path in love and work out his own salvation
with care. The process of transforming the feel-good physical, sexual love into
a higher, unconditional love takes gratitude for what you had and a lot of faith
and confidence in yourself. Call on all your muses to guide and inspire as you
release with love (if your heart and will is truly being challenged, carry out the
Code 13 spell which follows, but be careful).

More importantly, this act of grace and mercy frees you to receive the
blessings and love that had been blocked by the energy of this relationship. You
do know, however, that until nature takes her course—and that is for divine
timing to decree—you must not call him and try not to let your eyes meet.

If heaven made him, earth can find some use for him.
—ANCIENT CHINESE PROVERB

Code 13 Spell

A *t times, a goddess looking ahead* to the Celebration of love realizes that
to continue flowing and growing in her life with someone she truly
loves, she must gracefully dissolve any lingering burdens or detri-
mental distractions that cause doubt, fear, guilt, or self-sabotage. These burdens could be manifest as a habit, situation, or a person of the past or present

that causes considerable discomfort or pain. If you have honestly tried your best to heal the situation to no avail, call on the goddess.

This invocation should never be approached frivolously. Please be informed that once you give your concern to the universe, you have no say or power in how the avenging goddess Nemesis will roll the dice. You must be prepared to accept the Fates' *modus operandi*. Keep your intention silent.

- You will need a piece of paper, a black taper candle, preferably a disposable candlestick (a sculptured wad of tin foil works well), a black pen, and a permanent ink stamp that reads "canceled" (purchase it at an office supply store). Always begin this process on the first or second night after the full moon, the most conducive time for release.

- Write your "release request" lengthwise on the candle. After sunset, light the candle. (Either light the candle outside or near an open window to ventilate any wayward energy.) Write the same request on the paper, place it in the shadow of the candlelight, and repeat the following:

  Waning moon, wise and free,
  Bless and remove this burden from me.
  As this candle burns clear and bright,
  I release _____ to the moon tonight.

- Allow the candle to burn for thirteen minutes. Then take your "canceled" stamp and stamp the petition's request. Extinguish the flame. Fold the paper away from you, turn it, and again fold it away from you. Place it under the candlestick. Repeat the ritual for thirteen consecutive nights. On the last night (which should be the night before the new moon, an excellent time to begin anew), burn the petition, gather the ashes and remains of the candle, and bury it far from your home. Then say,

With blessings, so shall it be.

Now, let go and let goddess.

Words and Images of Passion

The Art of Sexual Magic by Margo Anand
The Art of Arousal by Dr. Ruth Westheimer
Delta of Venus: Erotica by Anaïs Nin
The *Kama Sutra*
On the Wings of Eros by Alicia Alvrez
Secrets of Seduction for Women by Brenda Venus
Soulful Sex by Dr. Victoria Lee

Love Tips

○ *Preserve the mystery.* Even if it seems averse to your molten desires, do not allow yourself to become "overexposed" during this season of Passion. Any wise goddess, or any famous movie star—just ask Greta Garbo—understands the value to being creatively elusive and naturally mysterious. When you are overexposed, you are drained of energy; when you feel depleted, your personal aura dims or becomes discolored; when you are all washed out, love is the last thing on your mind. The cycle is unrelenting. There's no need to accept every date, see him every day, or answer his calls every time. Only call him once every three days if that; write more love letters instead. Implementing subtle, teasing restrictions will in turn heighten the value of both of your desires. Pamper yourself with time to dream and revitalize and stay true to your goddess friends.

○ Breakfast dates are delicious. When at home, breakfast sybaritically on Key Lime Luna Pie topless while feeding each other with your eyes closed. Drink your juice straight from the fruit while your lover squeezes it. Be playful and let your imagination cater the event—always keep a tasty trick up your sleeve.

Invest in a giant umbrella and take languid strolls together in the rain. The supercharged negative ions in the atmosphere during this kind of weather can have the most amatory effect. Make love outdoors during a warm, summer rain. Make love spontaneously (indoors will suffice) during exhilarating thunderstorms to enhance passion, stamina, and feelings of lusty extravagance. If you are really adventurous, make love in a reputedly haunted inn or house at night during a storm. The energy will be wild.

Tame—or free—the green-eyed beast. Jealousy implies lack and self-pity ("Poor me, I don't have what I want; I want more attention, sniff, sniff"), and this runs against the current of everything that is sacred, abundant, and promising about love. When your self-confidence is receding with the waning moon and you are feeling feeble, lavish yourself with love and attention.

Embark on a feel-good fest of favorite activities alone or in the company of friends you admire. Give *zero* energy to the object of your envy. When the moon is in a water or earth sign, get a haircut and buy some new lipstick. There's truth to that goddess-based axiom, "Looking good is the best revenge." In other words, proclaims Ellen Patrick in *The Southern Rules*, "Be the most tantalizing girl at the barbecue."

⊘ Passion begets heat and any type of heat begets energy flare-ups, better known as arguments. Some confrontations concern the absurdly petty and some are deep and smoldering *à la* Pele—the unresolved issues within you will be manifested as conflicts between you and your beloved. But a goddess is wise enough to know we attract our problems because we need their gifts; a good, healthy row can clear the air like cosmic air spray.

Always try to *ascend*—be fair, listen, don't yell, and be nice. As a goddess, why not go one step further toward peace? This is the art of *The Sensuous Argument*: Take off your shirt and smile (always liberating!); get out a camera and document your lover's expressions for a picture show later; hold up a mirror; turn on a tape recorder. Instant peace—or at least quiet.

⊘ Make love in your car while listening to "Hotel California" by the Eagles, "Boys of Summer" by Don Henley, and Van Morrison's "Brown-Eyed Girl."

The Passion of love *transforms* you.

But at it's truest, love is altogether another matter:
a matter of gods and goddesses, or spirits merging,
of a holy communion in the flesh.
—ERICA JONG, *SERENISSIMA*

CHAPTER 5

The Celebration

The Grace of Autumn's Gifts

The Celebration Begins

For all that has been—Thanks!
For all that will be—Yes!
—MARY HEINTZ

It's time for the Celebration of love to begin. For some, the Celebration involves a pledge of commitment or a vow of marriage, for others it is blessed by the gifts of children or the creation of a home together. For others still, the season of Celebration includes a time of adventure, travel, and the security of knowing someone will always be waiting for you. For the goddess who is "self-blessed" with a heart free of bonds, the Celebration offers a time to be with admired friends who comfort and teach as the spirit of love grows stronger. The Celebration *always* involves the knowledge that love will be renewed with each season, with each new cycle of the moon, and each time you reconnect with the divine fire in your heart.

You are blissfully invited to a Celebration of your love! Refreshments of the soul will be served, laughter and entertainment will be provided, and gifts will be exchanged. Come frolic in the richness and bounty of hope's harvest, dance under the wise and waning beauty of the moon, and dwell on love's mysteries with delight. You will gather the wisdom from all seasons, dance in a mansion of mirth, and raise your praises to the Oktoberfest of Love! Regrets are not possible. Dreams and smiles are required. A place of esteem will be reserved for you and your beloved. Come . . . it is your season to *play in love*!

As the goddess of honor in your Celebration of love, you are the life-force of the party and the hostess, the mistress and the muse, the mentor and the matron. This, of course, requires a robust measure of timeless serenity, confidence, enthusiasm, and creative planning. In the spirit of any great party, the Celebration of love requires a bold theme, party favors, preparation, games, and enticements for the palate. It takes timing, preparation, and lots of free-flowing energy. You will want to look and feel your best, and you will want to be relaxed and regaled.

During this time of perfect balance between the elements of the universe and the forces of life—light and dark, night and day, knowing and learning, listening and speaking—the doyennes at the dance appear as abundance, prosperity, and stability. Traditionally governed by the province of water, the autumn equinox gifts you with the strength of equilibrium in love's ways and heralds the consummation of love's natural cycle. Great holiday banquets abound, for the harvest is in and flowing with nourishment, refreshment, and reserves for the future. The great goddesses of grace and equipoise saunter into the festivities, hostess gifts in hand. . . .

The Seven Gifts of the Goddess

1. *The Gift of Wisdom.* Your mind is illumined with intuitive knowledge and experience to feel, act, think, and speak in a divine and inspired way.

2. *The Gift of Understanding.* Your compassion for others and your interest in the splendor of all creation gives you the insight to embrace love's mystical purpose.

3. *The Gift of Bliss.* As a woman-child filled with awe and joy, you marvel at the glory and abundance of a goddess-graced universe.

4. *The Gift of Listening.* You are skilled at sharing one of the most priceless gifts one person can give another; the true listener is a golden soul.

5. *The Gift of Inspiration.* You are lavished with the divine guidance of the goddess through your dreams, your muses, your visions, and your love.

6. *The Gift of Strength.* You possess the will, resolve, determination, fortitude, and stamina necessary to free your heart to love.

7. *The Gift of Grace.* Your manner and choices dynamically avow that grace and beauty are essential to the progression of your soul.

Display these elegant gifts during every phase of every moon so long as you love. And remember, gifts by their nature are born to be shared. When the Seven Gifts of the Goddess become innately woven into your nature—your signature seal of being a goddess in love—and you begin to share them with others, joy will flow through your life like a wild mountain river and your lovelight will shine like a diamond in the noonday sun.

> *The ability to create magical relationships*
> *in your life begins and ends with you.*
> —WAYNE W. DYER, *REAL MAGIC*

The Balanced Dance of the Goddess

What comes to mind when you think of autumn? The colors of the countryside? Sharing weekend feasts and fun with family and friends? Thanksgiving? Most people will agree that when the fall wind picks up its tempo and the trees rustle in their brilliant finale of color, the rhythm of life itself begins to unwind and time seems to stretch with the afternoon shadows. Naturally, love relaxes with the days. The muses of spring and summer have strolled south where love and leaves are blooming in the southern hemisphere. In their honor, the tranquil goddesses of peace and promise reign over love's season of Celebration.

One of the most beloved goddesses in all the universe holds high court in the hearts of lovers in this exalted stage of divine romance. She is the mother of love, the embodiment of feminine wisdom and compassion, the Holy Rose, Queen of Heaven: she is Mary.

She is the inexperienced lover who says "Yes" when the angel of true love appears to her, who never judges others (after all, she *chose* to be pregnant though unwed—undoubtedly, tongues wagged), and who calls for understanding and gentle acceptance in the mysterious ways of love. She cautions you that love, like life, is so very, very, very fragile; its hope and innocence can be shattered with one word, one glance, one careless act. She promises you that "never was it known that anyone who implored her help or sought her intercession was left unaided." Amidst changes and challenges, she stands secure, her heart ever peaceful and glowing with divine light.

The Blessed Virgin Mary is also a very discerning goddess (she is the original Virgo; her feast day is September 8—the number and emblem of eternity) and she certainly knows important practical tactics in party planning. After all, it was she who hinted to her son, "They have no wine" (John 2:3). At this goddess' prompting, the first miracle was performed—water was turned into the finest wine—so the Celebration of love at Cana could continue.

Her soul sisters also shine in this season of love. Yemaya, "Star of the Sea," the beautiful and powerful Santéria goddess of the waters, counsels you in understanding your emotions and accepting love's natural ebb and flow. She remains tranquil, yet immensely powerful in any situation. Sarasvati, "the flowing one," Indian goddess of knowledge, the arts, music, and magic, emanates a brilliance that "destroys the darkness of ignorance." Calling her into your life and "drinking of her waters" purifies and nurtures your love and infuses you with divine energy in your union with your beloved.

In the Celebration of love, the Tibetan goddess of mercy and compassion, Tara, has the power to "grant all wishes and to heal all sorrows." Like her compatriot Mary, she comforts and aids those who beseech her help to overcome troublesome situations. In her presence, the fears that block harmony and happiness in love simply dissolve into a shining peace.

When you simply desire a little extra luck in love, invite Fortuna to take a spin with you for a spell. Originally a fertility goddess, let's simply say she found her "fortune" in her role as a goddess of prosperity. She turns the wheel of the year, the eternal cycle of love, the proverbial wheel of fortune, the lovers' wheel of emotional roulette. With a rudder in one hand, symbolizing her power to guide the destiny of the world, and a cornucopia of abundance in the other, Fortuna provides that precious surprise just when you think you know all there is to know about love.

> *A change of fortune hurts a wise person*
> *no more than a change of the moon.*
> —CHINESE PROVERB

Let's Play in Love!

By its inherent nature, true devotion in love is tender, sacred, and constant. But it is also dynamic, energized, and joyful. The Celebration of love reassures us that love can be renewed with the cycles of the seasons, with every new cycle of the moon, and with each new day. Life with your beloved can be savored with deep appreciation and delight! Isn't this the grandest reason of all to rejoice?

In the Celebration of love, your capacity to love and to be loved is forever evolving and changing; love's vitality is born of your charisma, will, and desires *in motion*. Taking a hint from physics, a goddess *in* love tends to *move in love* by running a lighter, more playful energy of divine bliss through her thoughts, words, and actions. In other words, a goddess doesn't *stay* in love, she *plays* in love.

Consider the word *stay—stop, pause, delay, stand still, remain, detain, suspend.* Why are lovers always pressured by society's unrealistic dictates and expectations to *stay* in love? Does this connote fulfillment and success to you? *Stay*. It brings to mind a lovely insect preserved in beautiful amber, nonetheless lifeless, petrified, stuck, soul-stifled.

In this light, toss away your doubts and fears about the need to stay in love. When playful progression and flourishing flow are the alternatives, why would you choose to stay in a suspended state of your once-upon-a-time chemically altered, romantic notion of love?

Create a unique love-style for your life-style. With cheerfulness and confidence, accept the new gifts given to you each and every day during the Celebration of love and learn to decorate your heart and life with the very best of these experiences. Enjoy yourself; you are a miracle. Exalt your beloved, a miracle as well. Dwell on your precious creation of love with delight—you are living a miracle conceived of miracles. Every day in every way aspire to reconnect with the divine fire in your heart and share this light with your lover; the more you give, the more you will have to give—a timeless secret to a life of golden love!

> *I'm off to be the wizard!*
> —ALAN COHEN

To thrive, love needs nourishment, attention, fresh air, and a lot of exercise just like any other living, breathing creation of life. Love needs rest and refreshment. To keep love alive, it is essential to regularly check its pulse.

By creating a *"love to"* checklist with your lover and updating it with each new season, you safeguard love by giving it the attention it deserves; you can then synchronize love's care and feeding program with its current development and appetite. Your commitment to personal happiness is renewed.

Beginning with the phrase "I love to. . . ," each person writes six to thirteen aspects of life—favorite activities, interests, desires, projects, ideas—that are most important to them *at that time* (the list, by love's nature, will change). Chronicle your lists in a special notebook and share the lists with each other. As you both tend to your love lists regularly, love will grow.

> *Change your "have to" thinking to "love to" thinking.*
> —SONIA CHOQUETTE

Feng Shui for Romance

In creating a nourishing environment to enhance and fortify love in all its seasons, a goddess in the know employs all the ancient secrets available to her—candle magic, meditation, creative spellcasting, and ultimately the powers of the elements and nature. In this light, *feng shui* (pronounced "fung shway", literally "wind and water") is the Cadillac of love enhancement.

This ancient Chinese art of cosmic interior (and often exterior) decorating focuses on cultivating and freeing an environment's natural *ch'i*—the life-force of the universe—by harnessing energy of objects, color, and elements. Through innovative placement of such reinforcements, you "marry" visible and invisible characteristics of energy, thus connecting the spiritual and physical worlds.

In *feng shui*, romance begins in the *yin* (feminine) vibration of your bedroom, the room of relationships. Therefore, to excite the *ch'i* in your relationship, make your bedroom a fortress of romance. Consider a few *feng shui* secrets shared by Chris Blanchard, *feng shui* goddess extraordinaire (available for consultation at 530-546-5999):

1. Enhance the far right corner (from the entrance) of your room with symbols that activate the *ch'i* of love: a dynamic photograph of you and your beloved, perhaps on vacation, laughing; a pair of something, like two candles or a sculpture of two animals or angels; any object that is heart-shaped; a well-placed, faceted crystal prism; a living, growing life-force, such as a plant

(remember to water it, of course); and mobile objects, a water fountain or a colorful mobile, to keep the *ch'i* in your heart moving.

2. Color is *ch'i's* cosmic consort. Is your love corner vibrating with red the quintessential color of passion? If it isn't, where is the passion in your romance? Decorate this area with vibrant objects, scarves, or paintings predominant in hues of red, pink, or garnet, accented in white (a little purity always helps).

3. Your bed, the bedding, and the location of your bed in the room are extremely important. You want a sturdy bed (stability in love) that is positioned up off of the floor, allowing *ch'i* to circulate around it (better sex!). The bed should be placed in the "commanding position" of the room, the far corner opposite the door, to insure feelings of safety and well-being in the relationship. And always invest in new linens—and a new mattress if at all possible—when you welcome a new lover. A goddess knows that displaced vibrations of a former paramour do not conduit constructive *ch'i*.

4. Bid farewell to all clutter in your room (and your relationship). Yes, this includes all those dried (dead) flowers from past Valentine's Days or even your wedding. At least put them in another room.

Remembering the Romance

There's rosemary, that's for remembrance:
Pray love, remember.
—SHAKESPEARE, OPHELIA IN *HAMLET*

After you have feng shui'ed your love life, slip back into quiet bliss, shut your eyes, and contemplate the happiest day or days of your life for a few minutes. What words come to mind—*enchanting, fascinating, captivating, triumphant, lusty, free?* What color do you see? What do you smell? All of these sensations of the soul combine to create memory. *Your* memory—another wondrous gift when thinking of all things beautiful about love. In the Celebration phase of love, memory acts as a bridge across which your heart can travel from the past to the future while delighting in the making of memories, new awakenings of the senses.

This season of love is fortified by playful scents such as citrus and gardenia, aromas that stimulate like rosemary (which also protects against evil and injury) and geranium, and the smells that inspire and soothe—neroli, myrrh, and frankincense. Wisely embrace the powers of these essences to open the mind and heart to the bounty in life. In addition to perfuming her aura, a goddess in love also adorns herself with her fairest finery of the season ("gild the bird," as my aunt advised) in her clothes, gems, and colors.

Adornment inspires a woman to feel good about herself, thus softening the more challenging aspects of the sometime demanding, often mundane, aspects of life. In the season of love's Celebration, wearing anything blue, purple, amber, or gold will embolden an attitude of gracefulness and power.

Claim your radiance—a goddess loves, pampers, and enhances the beauty of her physical body. Though a goddess naturally aspires to physical radiance, just as flower is drawn toward the sun, it is also very important to accept and love your body as it is. Concentrate on your best attributes. Love and care for your body unconditionally. If you find yourself succumbing to faultfinding, silence that critical voice immediately (self-criticism manifests *more* burden) and whisper aloud:

> *My body is strong, vibrant, and healthy;*
> *I am a masterpiece in progress.*
> *Love flows through every cell;*
> *I love and honor my body unconditionally.*

Then hug yourself and surrender all feelings of limitation and lack to the goddess. You are loved just the way you are.

Tanzanites Are a Goddess' Best Friend

Yes, diamonds are also our best friend—and for reasons not visible to the eye. A goddess attuned to Earth evokes the elemental energies of her stones and gems to enhance all aspects of love and life. Always cleanse your baubles initially in salt water and then wear them well! My pet rocks include:

Amethyst	Enhances spirituality; protects from addiction and over-indulgence; bestows strength, stability, and peace.
Diamond	Ensures love and harmony if freely given and worn with sincere intention; brings unity and confidence; amplifies emotion.
Rose Quartz	Banishes anger; removes negativity; heals emotional wounds; reinstates love and harmony after chaos.
Yellow Sapphire	Stimulates vivacity; attracts wealth and prosperity; brings fulfillment; enhances endurance and wisdom.
Tanzanite	"Stone of magic"; aids in manifestation; enhances psychic powers; facilitates telepathic communication; attracts divine revelations.

Will and Wisdom

The serenity and joyfulness experienced within the Celebration of love freely opens the goddess gates of the solar plexus and crown chakras. When the solar plexus (located in the stomach area) is empowered, your will is indefatigable—emotions of guilt, fear, and doubt are consumed by an instinctive awareness of personal worth. As with all chakras, you can activate your energy through focused stimulation of the senses—color, aromatherapy, touch, and taste. Eat foods that are fresh, wholesome, and brilliantly colored, such as papayas, sweet potatoes, carrots, oranges, and fish. The solar plexus asserts, "I will."

Renaissance painters depicted the crown chakra as a halo, an actual, visible light over the heads of the enlightened and inspired. A goddess is intimate with this subtle energy point—the crown chakra—the goddess gate that opens directly to the divine flow of love from the highest, most sacred source. When you begin to see a halo above your head or over the brow of your lover, you will know the crown chakra is spinning with the wisdom of love's mysteries.

The Crowning Blessing

To love someone is to believe in their best self and inspire them to let this self flourish. The Crowning Blessing offers a simple ritual to weave a spell of peace, grace, and gratitude into the psyche of your beloved. Adapted from traditional folk prayer offered for the living, extended family, this sacred acknowledgment of your devotion has the power to revitalize love in any of its seasons. Hold your hands over the crown chakra of your beloved and recite :

To my beloved _____
May the blessings of the goddess melt upon your forehead;
May you be your best self;

May your heart glow with peace and love;

May you walk in beauty;

May your path be guarded by angels;

May you be embraced with honor wherever you go;

May the light of the spirit fill your soul.

You are loved.

You are free.

Let the Spirit Move You

A superb way to relax when caught in the momentum of love's Celebration is to try your hand at automatic cooking. Like the clandestine Victorian-era divination art, automatic writing, this freeform approach to cooking involves a trusting release to the process. Our romantic predecessors, the Victorians—and the inspired wordsmiths after them—believed that the spirits would move the hand when a person was in a transcendent state of surrender, thus revealing unknown desires, secrets, and facts.

Undoubtedly, the kitchen spirits are also eager to move the spoon and aid us at our craft. My Victorian consultant, Lady Margaret (a.k.a. Peggy Tavener), has shared the perfect recipe for a virgin journey into automatic cooking. So when you cavort to the table with your culinary creations in hand, your focus is to dish up favorite endorsements of enchantment and satisfaction—forego tedious details and have fun!

Lady Margaret's Baked Potato Soup

2 large baking potatoes, baked with peels on

1½ pounds potatoes, peeled and diced

4 cups chicken broth, divided

½ pound bacon, chopped

1 large onion, minced

2 stalks celery, chopped

6 cloves garlic, minced

2 cups milk

½ cup butter

2 tablespoons fresh parsley, finely chopped

1 teaspoon crushed thyme

½ teaspoon spicy mustard

¼ cup sherry

Salt and a combination of white and black pepper

Garnishes of grated cheddar cheese, chopped fresh chives, remaining
half of crisp bacon bits, sour cream, and parsley sprigs

Bake two potatoes at 350° F for 40 minutes or until cooked through.

In a large soup pot, boil the diced potatoes in 3 cups of chicken broth until tender. Remove from heat and mash potatoes in the broth they were boiled in.

Fry chopped bacon until crisp; drain, divide in half, and set aside. Sauté onion, celery, and garlic in bacon drippings for several minutes.

Drain and dispose of grease. Add remaining broth, milk, butter, parsley, thyme, mustard, and sherry and bring to a boil over medium heat (and a watched pot), stirring often. Dice baked potatoes with peelings on and add to soup. Reduce to simmer and cook soup for another 20 to 30 minutes, stirring occasionally.

Serve with grated cheese, chopped fresh chives, sprinklings of the remaining bacon, and sour cream. Garnish with a sprig of parsley. The soup keeps quite well (Lady Margaret claims it seasons beautifully with time), refrigerated, for up to three days. Makes 6 to 8 servings—a weekend love feast!

> *My soul is satisfied as with a rich feast.*
> —PSALMS 63:5

A Goddess' Gift to the Gods

Sustenance delivered, the goddess of the house can relax, unfettered, and take "consummate delight in the pleasures of the table," namely sharing a cup of dark-roasted coffee, nibbling Perugina chocolate with your beloved, and whipping up this ambrosial, fresh-spirited cake when his sweet tooth gets frisky.

Kitty's Classic Carrot Cake

1 cup sugar

4 eggs, room temperature

2 teaspoons pure vanilla extract

1 cup vegetable oil

1 teaspoon salt

1 tablespoon ground cinnamon

1 teaspoon ground allspice

½ cup buttermilk

2 cups unbleached flour

2 teaspoons baking soda

4 cups peeled and finely grated carrots

1 cup crushed pineapple, drained

1 cup raisins

1½ cup pecans, chopped

Preheat oven to 350° F. Grease two 9-inch round baking pans.

In a large mixing bowl, beat the sugar, eggs, vanilla, oil, salt, and spices together. Blend the soda into the flour, then alternately mix in flour and buttermilk. Fold in carrots, pineapple, raisins, and nuts.

Pour this colorful batter into prepared pan and bake for 20 to 25 minutes until toothpick comes out clean or cake springs back when pressed with your finger. Cool and frost (recipe follows). Makes two 9-inch round pans, one 13 x 9 x 2-inch pan (baking time: 40 to 45 minutes) or a dozen cupcakes (baking time: approximately 20 minutes).

"Icing on the Cake" Butter-Cream Frosting

$1/2$ pound sweet butter, softened

6 cups powdered sugar

$1\frac{1}{2}$ teaspoons pure vanilla extract

$1/2$ cup plus 2 tablespoons half & half or milk

$1/2$ teaspoon lemon juice, optional

With an electric mixer on low speed, cream the butter, sugar, vanilla, and lemon juice. Slowly add the half & half or milk until the frosting is creamy. Beat well but do not overmix or the frosting will separate and clump. Ice your cake and enjoy it too! Will frost one 9-inch two-layer cake, one dozen cupcakes, or a 13 x 9 x 2-inch cake.

Always preheat; then have fun.
—JUNE SYLVESTER

Creating a Goddess Box

Your dreams and desires need a place of divine repose where they can germinate and grow. The Goddess Box provides a microcosm of your life, supported by your attentions and intentions, where the true law of love and abundance can work its magic.

To create a Goddess Box, attract a box or container of your liking with a lid you can close, like a hatbox, a shoebox, a little wooden chest, or a large cookie tin. Cleanse it with salt water and consecrate it with a favorite essential oil such as cinnamon oil for attraction or rose essence for love. Decorate it—inside and out—with images, words, and colors that represent you— your passions and interests, photographs of people who inspire you, pictures of places that intrigue or energize you (I have a photograph of me, healthy and smiling, in the French Riviera and an image of the Notre Dame football stadium—a childhood feel-good haven—in mine). Be creative, shine your box up with imagination and love and release its magic with objects of your desire.

On each new moon, after you've done the New Moon Meditation (see page 36), place your written intentions in your Goddess Box. You may also write your dearest and deepest heart's desires in purple ink on a beautiful piece of paper and surrender it to the goddess via your magic box. Close the lid and place your Goddess Box near a window where the rays of moonlight can bathe it. (If you have no such window, take it outside occasionally to be energized.) As your dreams material-ize, take the love note with your particular dream-come-true from the Goddess Box, and write "Thank you" on it. Finally, with your dream as guest of honor, throw a personal celebration of gratitude.

Goddess' Manifestation Management

The single most important skill to acquire during this season of love is the art of what I call "Manifestation Management." By now you have become a mistress of enlisting the favors of the Fates, knowing how to create, entice, emblazon, and inspire love in its multifaceted splendor. You know that the alchemical solution to any problem is love in motion. You know that the secret to loving is loving. Yet, unless you learn to preside over your creations like the graceful goddess-queen you are, your empire is vulnerable.

As a respectful example of a tragic lack of Manifestation Management, think about Princess Diana. She knew the secrets to attracting her prince; it is said, as a teenage goddess she hung photographs of her future beloved on her walls. She knew her power; she visualized a life of adoration. She created her masterpiece (and the throne's heirs) and we all cheered.

However, somewhere in her seasons of love, she began playing by mortal rules. Succumbing to the relentless demands and pressures of others' expectations—not her own—she lost touch with her goddess power. The triple goddess of maiden-mother-mentor—will, love, and wisdom—eluded her. And when she finally did recognize the smiling, loving soul of the goddess within her once again, the Fates arrived. And, as you know, or *should* know, no goddess nor god has "cosmic exemption" from the decisions of the Fates.

The Golden Goddess Rule

In order to successfully bask in the glory of your heart's accomplishments, you must be deeply appreciative of the love you have in your life and not allow a day to pass where you do not honor it in some way. Not a day, goddesses, not a day. The very essence of your nature must emanate the universal Golden Goddess Rule: *Love others the way you would want them to love you.*

Truly acknowledge how you like to be treated, cherished, and respected and mirror this compassion when considering the feelings of another. Let the sincerity of your intentions and respect for love *be what you do.* When you are able to apply the Golden Goddess Rule effortlessly and lucidly, you develop a "sympathetic resonance" with your lover, an ability to communicate in ways that delve deeper than words or actions.

When you do converse with words, strive to listen more than you talk. Listening is a rare and strong skill. Truly listening to your lover empowers and comforts him, freeing inner silences and diminishing discomfort and fear. Behavioral psychologists assert that listening, as a positive reinforcement, is more effective than rewards of sex, food, and money. Listening's closest contender for infusing a sense of accomplishment in your lover is laughter. Consider it is scientifically proven: Listening and laughter are more motivating than promises of sex!

Freedom and intimacy are to a person what sun and water are to a plant; both must be present at the same time for a person to flourish. Allow your mate the freedom to enjoy his interests, hobbies, athletic pursuits, and his friends. And certainly see that he reciprocates in this dance of respect. Your beloved must support you in pursuing your dreams, caring for your friends, and nurturing your goddess-spirit. You must appreciate each other.

I have come to think listening is love,
that's what it really is.
—BRENDA UELAND

Gracefully Dissolving Conflict

When attempting to overcome blocks in love's flow, always keep this goddess-tip in mind: If what you have been doing hasn't worked, doing more of the same isn't likely to work, either. If your feelings about love ever become so muddled or tangled you are in despair, *love more*. Then, make a change—change *yourself* for the better.

Step back; get rid of the adrenalin rush of anxiety; stop stirring up the mud puddle. Then, give yourself a spiritual massage of the senses and get grounded (pull yourself together!). Learn to be *proactive* and not *reactive*. When someone says something that ruffles you, count to thirteen (ten may not be enough; the extra three seconds have magic in them) before you respond.

You are responsible for producing, directing, and starring in your own love story; hopefully it is a four-star classic and not a B-rated soap opera. A goddess in love knows that peace is an achieved state—she never allows herself to laze and become comfortable in an area of conflict. Embrace your creation with tenderness. Give your love new life, every morning, every day.

Serious Moon Power

A goddess cannot speak of love without speaking of being a woman. And being a woman is inseparable from the tides and flows of the body. Invariably, this flow has an attitude of its own: many call it PMS, premenstrual syndrome. During this time (which I describe as SMP—Serious Moon Power—I do not subscribe to the PMS cliché) a woman must employ the wisdom of ages such as herbalism, massage, meditation, relaxation, sleep, and dreamtime, and allow her body to flow with its natural potency.

She must indulge herself in the company of loving friends, avoid chemicals that may impair her vision, such as too much alcohol, and embrace the process of being a woman. A goddess in love is also sensitive to the benightedness of her beloved during SMP—men simply will never truly comprehend the flux of this matter; many women don't fully understand its profound effects.

Please understand. I am not discounting the fact that you honestly feel irritable and uncomfortable, and experience the pain of headaches or cramps. I also realize that it is not a figment of your somewhat hormone-laced imagination that pounds have appeared on your scale. But I also believe that calling this "premenstrual syndrome" is a disturbing sign of our times and our society's view of women's processes. A very powerful time of *natural*, feminine physiological and psychological transition has been labeled a disease and many women have chosen to become its victim.

To my amazement, I know women who have agreed to take Prozac or go on the Pill to avoid the "menace" of PMS. I feel they are refusing to confront the intensity of their own senses, and consequently the force of the goddess surging within them. We must reclaim the power of our menstrual cycles, learn from our bodies' wisdom, nourish them gently and lovingly, and work *with* them.

As goddesses, if we reject the "curse" of PMS and choose to venerate the existence of SMP in its place, our internal conflicts will subside; eventually then, this techno-modern "disease" of women who have lost connection with their sacred moontime power will cease—as will a lot of senseless, hormone-blamed arguments with our mates.

> *And I, understanding what you did not say,*
> *fell in love with you because you did not say it.*
> —GUERRINI

It's time to escort the troublemakers at love's Celebration to the door. Call on a wise and savvy goddess to act as cosmic bouncer and show them out as soon as possible. Believe me, love won't miss these party-poopers for one molecule of a second—*ever*.

Mrs. Senseless Anger

Mr. Judgment

Ms. Doubt

Mr. Fear

Mrs. Taking for Granted

Mr. Dead-End

Mr. and Mrs. Guilt and Guilt-Tripping

Mr. Low Esteem

Miss Envy

Mrs. Possessiveness

Mr. Addiction

Ms. Dishonesty

Hallowed Be Thy Name

As the light of the moon retreats for rest, and the vibrancy of the season winds down, love reposes willingly. As with every great celebration, there comes a time when you welcome the party's finale; you are ready to pull the wishbone. You look forward to settling back and savoring the memories; the sights, the entertainment, and shared, happy moments. It's time to go rest your heart and head. For when you slumber, you dream, and when you dream, the mysterious power of the goddess comes to refresh you. In this post-party stillness you enter into her realm, the odd and shadowed dance on the other side of the looking glass.

The centuries-old, elaborate rituals and festivals of All Hallows evolved to synthesize and embrace, and sometimes defy, the intensely transformative aspects of this season. It was during this ancient Celtic fire festival of *Samhain* (pronounced "sow-ain") that rituals such as lighting bonfires and giving treats to visitors were created to lend protection from evil, the invisible, and the wayward souls wandering in the Underworld's labyrinth.

The sand in the hourglass is running thin, calling for complete release of that which no longer serves and heralding a new year, a new phase, a return. Understanding and honoring the mystery of this season is essential to ensure the continuation of the circle of life and the subsequent resurrection and renewal of love.

This enchanted holiday is also reserved for fervent spiritual reflection, foretellings, high magic, and potent refreshment. During these high holy days of love's Celebration, a goddess craves the richness and remedial connection of her ancient customs and rites, because through them she becomes divinely human for a twinkling of time. And this is the time for love.

> *Mutual love, the crowning bliss.*
> —JOHN MILTON

Sixty Seconds of Gratitude

eing grateful for the gifts you have been given, love being the most resplendent of all, is the very foundation of a timeless, joyous Celebration of life. For the love you give *and* the love you receive to thrive with freshness, stability, and magic, always count your blessings and gifts. A careless rain falls on the party whose revelers are numb with the side-effects of living in a fast-forward world. If you don't make the effort to protect your lovelight with an umbrella of gratitude, your light will dim or be extinguished.

Make a promise to yourself to consciously set aside a time each day (even if it is but sixty precious seconds) to fortify your belief in the miracle of love; keep the river of your soul flowing with clear and clean waters through the practice of gratitude. Upon waking, as you lie in bed drifting through your dreams, greet the glory of the new day with a sacred declaration of the power of love. Either with your lover or by yourself, aloud or in silence, recite this personal Celebration of rebirth, new beginnings, and possibilities inspired by an Irish prayer, or create a canticle—and a time—of your own:

> *I arise this day*
> *With love in my heart,*
> *Through the warmth of the sun,*
> *The radiance of the moon,*
> *Freedom of the wind,*
> *Joy of rushing water,*
> *Splendor of fire,*

Stability of earth,
Serenity of stars, and
the wisdom of silence.

I embrace this day
Through the grace of the goddess to guide me
And the promise of love to inspire me.

Words of Celebration

"Phenomenal Woman" by Maya Angelou

"Desiderata" by Max Ehrmann

The Secret of Staying in Love by John Powell

A Lifetime of Love by Daphne Rose Kingma

Communication Miracles for Couples by Jonathan Robinson

Heart Centered Marriage by Sue Patton Thoele

Simple Abundance by Sarah Ban Breathnach

She is a friend of my mind.
She gather me, man. The pieces I am, she gather them and
give them back to me in all the right order. It's good, you know,
when you got a woman who is a friend of your mind.
—TONI MORRISON, *BELOVED*

Love Tips

❡ Become an expert, à la *déesse*—"in the style of the god-dess," in your favorite field. This adds zest to any relation-ship. Possible titles include that of *Thaumatologist*—goddess who studies the existence and creation of miracles; *Balneologist*—a goddess of the bath who studies the thera-peutic use of various sorts of bathing, as in mineral springs; *Psychometrist*—a goddess who can feel the vibra-tions of a specific person by holding or observing a materi-al item the person touched, such as a watch, necklace, or of the vibrations of objects; *Une Flaneuse*—a goddess who has mastered the art of strolling idly, as in, along the boulevards; *Oneironaut*—an unabashed dreamer.

❡ Learn what "Touchdown Jesus" means in football. A god-dess honors the fact that viewing and engaging in sports, which are based on ancient traditions of displaying and competing for women's attentions, are sacred ceremonies for the male of the species. A wise women respects this aspect of her beloved and encourages his enthusiasm. Enlighten yourself with a copy of Joe Theismann's *The Complete Idiot's Guide to Understanding Football Like a Pro* and you'll understand why players invoke the goddess with a "Hail Mary" during some games.

Practice writing haikus to your lover. A haiku is a Japanese poem rendered in English as three unrhymed lines of five, seven, and five syllables, respectively (for a total of seventeen syllables). Haikus are "composer-friendly" little poems and can be tantalizing, romantic, and mysterious at the same time. Here's an example:

Windy love afar
friend of many distances
the jackstraw quivers

Moonlight mountain night
laughter echoes in my heart
smiling eyes kiss me

Learn to pray. For every religious cosmology there is a different method of communicating with the powers that be and for every description of the deed, there is a different word—*pray, creatively visualize, invoke, implore, beseech, meditate, attract*. Regardless, "it is the pleasure of the universe to give us what we need," so praying is always win-win. Though you are asking for divine assistance, you become an active ingredient in your creation by knowing who you are, what you want, and what you will do when you are given the answer to your request. In *A Book of Angels,* Sophy Burnham outlines a very simple and unquestionably effective approach to prayer:

Ask—Phrase your prayer in a positive, present tense, free of all doubt, and conclude with a phrase of surrender to universal will, such as "So be it, or better," "Thy will be done," or something to that effect;

Notice—Simply stated, greet the answer when it arrives, welcome it into your life, and move with it;

Respond—Always say "Thank you" and smile;

Release—Share your gift.

Using the freshest ingredients in your kitchen will often inspire you to use a fresher approach to love in your life. Like the grandma-goddess says, "Like bread, love must be baked fresh every day." Purge your cupboards of clutter, outdated goods, "dead" spices, and unhealthful foods. Fresh spices add vitality to a dish, producing a more flavorful, delicate, and alluring taste. Plant an herb garden, however small; city goddesses can grow spice gardens of Italian parsley, sage, rosemary, thyme, sweet basil, and chives in a window box. You've heard it before, "Add spice to life!"

Sing a favorite song out loud that conveys your feeling of love's Celebration. I always hear Sidney Poitier's character in the classic movie *Lilies of the Field* singing a song at the end; as he packs his car to go, he's grateful, he's satisfied, and he recognizes it is time to roll with the seasons. His heart is blazing with joy. Remember that song? O.K. Now, clap your hands and sing with me:

A-men, a-men . . . a-men, a-men, a-men (Sing again!)

A-men, a-men . . . a-women, a-women, a-women (Sing it louder!)

A-woman, a-woman . . . a-women, a-women, a-women! (Sing on!)

The Celebration of love *frees* you!

> *Faring thee well now,*
> *Let your life proceed by its own design.*
> —JOHN BARLOW, "CASSIDY"

CHAPTER 6

The Secret to Playing in Love

*For the spirit that is blissful,
whatever happens to us is flawless. . . .*

—RILKE

Goddess to Goddess

You are a goddess now. You have done a cosmic cartwheel over the out-dated paradigm of love, have donned prescription-strength rain-bow-tinted goddess glasses, and have a joyful, pristine, crystal-clear vision of love in your soul. You have embraced your feminine connection with the moon, nourished your psyche, and have swung open your heart to the divine mystery of the universal power of the playground called love.

As a goddess, you know the secret to *playing in love* relies on your ability to draw on the timeless wisdom and flow of the natural cycles of the seasons, the moon, and the tempo of the universe for guidance and strength, balance, and completeness. Openly call on the goddess—your muse, your mother, your mistress, your mentor—for intimate inspiration. You now realize that love can wax and wane, month to month, season to season, like the capricious moon in her eternal, brilliant dance. You color your world with the shades and desires of the season, perfume your dreams with the essences of the world that caresses you, and honor the sensual, sexual power of your body in ecstasy.

Like the seasons of the year and the light of the moon, each natural phase of love—the Vision, the Enchantment, the Passion, the Celebration—holds a secret and a gift for you. The Vision of love rekindles the lovelight in your heart and empowers you with the wisdom of winter's stillness; you emerge enlight-ened, grounded, and attractive to love. The playfulness and promise of love's Enchantment reminds you that love, like spring, is eternal; you are inspired to open your heart with faith and trust in love.

The Passion of love transforms you. Buoyant and wise, you ascend in love toward summer's lusty fireball of emotion, and rather than fly into the flame, you dance around it, over it, and beyond. As the circle of love encompasses your heart, you rejoice in the Celebration of love's fruits. Your spirit flows with grace and understanding and you bask in the fulfillment of a dream. You are free to love.

Love in Motion

Do something extraordinary every day. Next time it rains, go out into the rainshower, close your eyes, turn your face to the sky, smile, and make a wish for yourself. Love is that rainstorm and love is the rainbow. You will never again be persuaded that there is anything wrong with getting wet if it feels good to you. Just listen to that little voice in the center of your soul because it knows what you need to be happy; your intuition will *never* mislead you. Attract. Ascend. Play!

Have more fun—laugh more, love freely, stay in bed all day if you want, eat chocolate for breakfast, kiss your beloved on the forehead more often—and be grateful for what you have. By regarding love as a force that is alive and in motion, you breathe vitality into it. If you practice *loving* (just as you would practice any talent you wished to develop—playing the piano, dancing the tango, or riding a horse) as often as possible, the "goddess gate" of your heart will open and your life will change. Every cell in your entire body and being will respond; you—and your love—will shine with the luminescence of a light infused with divine vibrance. I promise you.

Free to Love

My dream in sharing these timeless secrets of divine love is not to *inform* but to *inspire*—not to give you information, but to give you hope. I truly believe you already hold all the answers to the mystery of love in your heart. Now you must call on your courage, give yourself a loving hug, and step forward to unlock those doors. Whether or not you'll be able to recognize your heart's desire when you stand face to face with it—your ideals, your dreams, and yourself—depends on your awareness and insight.

Are you able to love yourself? Are you ready to love and to be loved by others? Are you willing to risk every preconceived notion of what love is *supposed* to be in order to discover what love really *is*? These are the only three questions you will ever need to ask yourself; and there is only one word that will ignite a life of love. The rest is choice . . . and always trust your choices.

If you ever find yourself in a difficult moment, look up to the sky and feel the power of love written all over the universe—in the moon, the clouds, the sunshine, the breeze, the trees, and the stars. Kneel down and place the palm of your hand, fingers spread wide, on the ground and feel the power of love flow through your body. You are never alone. You are loved. Hear the goddess whisper to you, *"To everything there is a season, and a time for every purpose under heaven."* Believe it. Believe in the goddess. Believe in yourself.

> *You don't need to leave your room.*
> *Remain sitting at your table and listen.*
> *Don't even listen, simply wait.*
> *Don't even wait.*
> *Be quite still and solitary.*
> *The world will freely offer itself to you.*
> *To be unmasked, it has no choice.*
> *It will roll in ecstasy at your feet.*
> —FRANZ KAFKA

Written Wisdom for the Goddess in Love

If I suggested all the books that could bring insight and knowledge and enhance the love and wonder in your life, the list would be longer than this book. Therefore, I've included some of my favorites— books that, as I see them, illuminate a path that is quite possibly "the shortest distance between two points" on the wise woman's journey.

About Love by Robert C. Solomon

The Art of Sexual Ecstasy by Margo Anand

Ask Your Angels by A. Daniel, T. Wyllie, and A. Ramer

A Book of Pagan Rituals

Creating Sacred Space with Feng Shui by Karen Kingston

The Five Love Languages by Gary Chapman

The Holy Book of Women's Mysteries by Zsuzsanna E. Budapest

Jambalaya: The Natural Woman's Book of Personal Charms and Practical Rituals by Luisah Teish (a favorite!)

Llewellyn's Annual Magical Almanac

Living the Tarot by Amber Jayantri

The Modern Book of Feng Shui by Steven Post

The Only Astrology Book You'll Ever Need by Joanna Martine Woolfolk

The Precious Present by Spencer Johnson, M.D.

Parker's Astrology by Julia and Derek Parker

The Pleasure Zone by Stella Resnick

The Rules (read this for fun, like going to the zoo; these "creatures like no others" are mating in captivity, but it's an interesting anthropological study for a goddess!)

Sacred Living by Robin Heerens Lysne

Secrets About Men Every Woman Should Know by Barbara De Angelis

Sex Tips for Straight Women from a Gay Man by Dan Anderson and Maggie Berman (a Bacchanalian classic!)

Sexual Bewitchery by B. Dolnick, J. Condon, and D. Limoges

Sexual Personae by Camille Paglia (persevere, it's worth it)

Sun Signs, Love Signs, and *Star Signs,* all by Linda Goodman

True Success by Tom Morris

A Victorian Grimoire by Patricia Telesco (appendix includes magical goods' resources and glossary of magical terms)

The Whole Truth About Contraception by Beverly Winikoff, M.D., M.P.H., and Suzanne Wymelenberg (fertility rights!)

The Women's Encyclopedia of Myths and Secrets by Barbara G. Walker

The Women's Spirituality Book by Diane Stein

The World of Aromatherapy edited by Jeanne Rose and Susan Earle (includes an extensive resource list for oils and more)

Most works by Tom Robbins, Erica Jong, Daphne Rose Kingma, Dr. Ruth Westheimer, Rainer Maria Rilke, Alan Cohen, D. H. Lawrence, Sophy Burnham, Colette, Sark, Gregory J. P. Godek, and Shakespeare.

May the call of the goddess
keep your mind emblazoned with light and grace,
and may your lovelight continue to shine
as you flow through your seasons of love and life.
Stay in touch!

A LAST WORD

ove is elusive, yet ever present. Love is a mystery. Love is an eternal theme, the organizing principal of the universe. Indeed, the entire cultural evolution of our species can be seen as a quest for love. Love will always be our most consuming need and activity.

This book very gently teaches us new ways of loving. This is important, for we must learn to love well, each generation on its own, in order to build a more loving culture.

A lack of love creates sickness in the soul, but no one can "will" love; love will or will not happen. This book focuses on love with a partner, but love is also present in solitude, when you understand that you are always part of the Beloved. When we dedicate ourselves to a higher goal of loving everyone, we realize that feeling truly alive is being in love. Being in love with life is the highest bliss. Separation is illusionary; all dying people know this when they see, many for the first time, that all is one. One love created everything.

Knowing this brings peace. To be greatly pleased is to be happy; to be greatly happy is to be in bliss. And to be in bliss is to be truly alive.

—Z BUDAPEST, AUTHOR OF *GODDESS IN THE BEDROOM*

ACKNOWLEDGMENTS

To Vojko and Lila, my best friends;

To Kimberly Terrell, who has inspired me more than ramblings of love and "goddess soup" can tell;

To Mary Jane Ryan, the archangel of this book's annunciation, for her love of the word, her faith, and her editing magic; to Brenda Knight for her sensuous vision; to Claudia Schaab for her flawless presence; to Ame Beanland for her touch of beauty; to Sharon Donovan for her energy and voice; and to everyone in Conari's playground of the goddess.

To Michael Joseph Beiser, may you bask in the happiness of pursuit, the grace of the BVM, the glory of a Lila smile, the pride in your baby "twin-sistar," and your translation of Rilke; and thank you for sneaking a copy of *The Happy Hooker* to me when I was a teenage virgin goddess;

To Dorismarie Welcher, Queen of the Hudson, who reminded me, "Remember Margie, Edward VIII abdicated the throne for 'it'";

To Shivani Grail Atkinson, Goddess of Manifestation, who has inspirited me with her message and the zest of her herbal delights;

To my muses, "Sistar" Kate and Mom, Paula Wilson, Kelly Douglass, Chyrise Broyer Porter, Ambrosia Healy, Cassidy Law, Linda D. Graber, Kathryn Grenda, Kitty Smith, Joanie Calhoon Schwartz, Colleen O'Brien, Grace Fuller, Linda Azar, Dr. Nicole Noyes, and Mary Heintz, my godmother;

To Patrice Patterson Parsons, my energized attaché;

To Liz Buckley and Diane Cutler for their healing hands, hearts, and loving tubfuls of Sacred Salts (essential to my research as Goddess of the Bath);

To those I love;

To Notre Dame and Dad;

And in memory of Diana Spencer, Diana, Princess of Wales, whose life, compassion, and deliverance inspired many to love and granted me a profound glimpse at the creation of a goddess-myth in my lifetime.

BIBLIOGRAPHY

Andrews, Lynn V. *Love and Power.* New York: HarperCollins, 1997.

Billings, Dr. Evelyn. *The Billings Method: Controlling Fertility Without Drugs or Devices.* New York: Random House, 1980.

A Book of Pagan Rituals. York Beach, ME: Samuel Weiser, Inc., 1978.

Blanchard, Chris. Personal Interview. April 4, 1998.

Bolen, Jean Shinoda. *Goddesses in Everywoman.* New York: Harper & Row, 1984.

Budapest, Zsuzsanna E. *The Goddess in the Bedroom.* New York: HarperCollins, 1995.

Cahill, Thomas. *How the Irish Saved Civilization.* New York: Anchor Books, Doubleday, 1995.

Choquette, Sonia. *The Psychic Pathway: A Workbook for Reawakening the Voice of Your Soul.* New York: Crown Trade Paperbacks, 1995.

_____.*Your Heart's Desire: Instructions for Creating the Life You Really Want.* New York: Three Rivers Press, 1997.

Cohen, Alan. *I Had It All the Time.* Haiku, HI: Alan Cohen Publications, 1995.

Collins, Terah Kathryn. *The Western Guide to Feng Shui.* Hay House, Inc., 1996.

Cunningham, Scott. *The Magic in Food: Legends, Lore and Spellwork.* St. Paul, MN: Llewellyn Publications, 1990.

Dolnick, Barrie, Julia Condon, and Donna Limoges. *Sexual Bewitchery and Other Ancient Feminine Wiles.* New York: Avon Books, 1998.

Dyer, Wayne W. *Real Magic: Creating Miracles in Everyday Life.* New York: HarperCollins, 1992.

Estes, Clarissa Pinkola. *Women Who Run with the Wolves.* New York: Ballantine Books, 1992.

Ferraro, Susan. *Sweet Talk: The Language of Love.* New York: Simon & Schuster, 1995.

Godek, Gregory J.P. *Love: The Course They Forgot to Teach You in School.* Naperville, IL: Casablanca Press, 1997.

Garrison, Omar. *Tantra: The Yoga of Sex.* New York: Julian Press, 1964.

Gonzalez-Wippler, Migene. *The Complete Book of Spells, Ceremonies and Magic.* St. Paul, MN: Llewellyn Publications, 1988.

Lapanja, Margie. *Goddess in the Kitchen.* Berkeley, CA: Conari Press, 1998.

Linn, Denise. *Sacred Space.* New York: Ballantine Books, 1995.

Lovric, Michelle. *How to Write Love Letters.* New York: Shooting Star Press, 1995.

Kelly, Sean, and Rosemary Rogers. *Saints Preserve Us!* New York: Random House, 1993.

Kingma, Daphne Rose. *A Lifetime of Love.* Berkeley, CA: Conari Press, 1998.

Melody. *Love Is in the Earth: A Kaleidoscope of Crystals.* Wheat Ridge, CO: Earth-Love Publishing House, 1995.

Moore, Thomas. *The Care of the Soul*. New York: HarperCollins, 1992.

Murdock, Maureen. *The Heroine's Journey*. Boston: Shambhala, 1990.

O'Hara, Gwydion. *The Magick of Aromatherapy*. St. Paul, MN: Llewellyn Publications, 1998.

Paglia, Camille. *Sexual Personae*. New York: Vintage Books, 1991.

Patrick, Ellen. *The Southern Rules: The Advanced Course for Women Who Are Serious About Taming the Male Beast*. Birmingham, AL: Sweet Water Press, 1997.

Pennick, Nigel. *The Pagan Book of Days*. Rochester, NY: Destiny Books, 1992.

Regula, deTraci. *The Mysteries of Isis*. St. Paul, MN: Llewellyn Publications, 1995.

Resnick, Stella. *The Pleasure Zone*. Berkeley, CA: Conari Press, 1997.

Robbins, Tom. *Still Life with Woodpecker*. New York: Bantam Books, 1980.

Rose, Jeanne. *Herbs and Aromatherapy for the Reproductive System*. Berkeley, CA: Frog, Ltd., 1994.

Rose, Jeanne, and Susan Earle, eds. *The World of Aromatherapy*. Berkeley, CA: Frog, Ltd., 1996.

Rossbach, Sarah. *Interior Design with Feng Shui*. New York: Penguin/Arkana, 1987.

Sills, Judith. *A Fine Romance*. New York: Ballantine Books, 1987.

Solomon, Robert C. *About Love: Reinventing Romance for Our Times*. New York: Touchstone, 1988.

Stein, Diane, ed. *The Goddess Celebrates.* Freedom, CA: The Crossing Press, 1991.

Stein, Diane. *The Women's Spirituality Book.* St. Paul, MN: Llewellyn Publications, 1987.

Teish, Luisah. *Jambalaya: The Natural Woman's Book of Personal Charms and Practical Rituals.* New York: Harper and Row, 1985.

Telesco, Patricia. *The Urban Pagan.* St. Paul, MN: Llewellyn Publications, 1993.

_____. *A Victorian Grimoire.* St. Paul, MN: Llewellyn Publications, 1992.

Theismann, Joe. *The Complete Idiot's Guide to Understanding Football Like a Pro.* New York: Alpha Books, 1997.

Ueland, Brenda. *Strength to Your Sword Arm: Selected Writings.* Duluth, MN: Holy Cow! Press, 1992.

Walder, Kris. *The Book of Goddesses.* Hillsboro, OR: Beyond Words Publishing, Inc., 1995.

Walker, Barbara G. *The Women's Encyclopedia of Myths and Secrets.* Edison, NJ: Castle Books, 1983.

_____. *Women's Rituals: A Sourcebook.* San Francisco: HarperSanFrancisco, 1990.

Woolfolk, Joanna Martine. *The Only Astrology Book You'll Ever Need.* Chelsea, MI: Scarborough House, 1990.

INDEX

A NOTE TO THOSE WHO LOVE

I welcome all love letters, questions, comments, and telepathic messages. I especially love hearing the story about your *first crush*—that innocent and passionate moment when *the magic* first stirred in your soul.

If you are interested in hosting a *Goddess' Guide to Love* "playshop" in your area or would like to contact me about a speaking engagement, please write me at:

GODDESS IN LOVE
c/o Margie Lapanja
Post Office Box 5515
Incline Village, Nevada 89450

If you liked this book, you'll also enjoy my book *Goddess in the Kitchen*— sure to enliven you with its spiritual-sensual tribute to the arts of cooking, loving, and living.

It is available at local bookstores or by calling 800-685-9595.

ABOUT THE AUTHOR

Margie Lapanja is author of Goddess in the Kitchen *and* a popular columnist who writes about the grand, captivating sources of life—food and love. She has been the *North Tahoe / Truckee This Week*'s restaurant critic for over six years and recently debuted as the magazine's love columnist with "Aphrodite's Afterthoughts."

A former professional baker who holds a degree in Humanities and Behavioral Science, Lapanja explores the aphrodisiacal effects of food on the psyche, body, and soul while teaching "playshops" on favorite topics at Sierra Nevada College.

As a visionary, voluptuary, and self-described ecstatician—a person skilled in the arts of bliss, beauty, and delight—she is dedicated to bringing more love, fun, and goddess-energy to this world by sharing her intuitive wisdom, rich experience, and practical magic (her baked creations, particularly "Margie's Cowboy Cookies," are deemed to possess special powers by those who have tasted them). She enjoys life at Lake Tahoe in Nevada with her husband-consort and their daughter, Lila.

Conari Press, established in 1987, publishes books
on topics ranging from spirituality and women's history to
sexuality and personal growth. Our main goal is to publish quality
books that will make a difference in people's lives—both how we
feel about ourselves and how we relate to one another.

Our readers are our most important resource, and we value
your input, suggestions, and ideas. We'd love to hear from you—
after all, we are publishing books for you!

For a complete catalog or to get on our mailing list,
please contact us at:

CONARI PRESS
2550 Ninth Street, Suite 101
Berkeley, California 94710

800-685-9595   Fax: 510-649-7190
conari@conari.com
www.conari.com